Dual-Career Marriage

Dual-Career Marriage

Conflict and Treatment

DAVID G. RICE, PH.D.
Professor of Psychiatry
University of Wisconsin Medical School

THE FREE PRESS
A Division of Macmillan Publishing Co., Inc.
NEW YORK

Collier Macmillan Publishers
LONDON

The Free Press
A Division of Macmillan Publishing Co., Inc.
866 Third Avenue, New York, N.Y. 10022

Collier Macmillan Canada, Ltd.

Library of Congress Catalog Card Number: 79–7179

Printed in the United States of America

printing number

1   2   3   4   5   6   7   8   9   10

Library of Congress Cataloging in Publication Data

Rice, David Gordon
    Dual-career marriage.

    Includes index.
    1. Married people--Employment--United States--
Psychological aspects. 2. Family psychotherapy.
I. Title.
HQ536.R465 1979   301.42   79-7179
ISBN 0-02-926380-8

To Joy, Scott,
and Andy,
my dual-career family

Contents

CONTENTS

Preface

MANY SOCIAL CRITICS believe that the contemporary institution of marriage is in trouble. The increasing divorce rate and the distancing of the nuclear from the extended family, common in a mobile society, to mention but a few examples, are cited to support claims of widespread marital breakdown. On the other hand, the present period is one in which individuals in alternative marital and family life-styles sense a freedom to develop and perhaps flourish. The most prevalent alternative marital life-style in contemporary American society is probably the dual-career marriage.

Like all couples, those in dual-career marriages face many stresses and strains. When initial attempts by the partners themselves to deal with problems are not successful, professional help is often sought. Perhaps as a result of the relative newness of dual-career relationships as a common marital pattern, there is little written from a clinical standpoint to help either the marital therapist or the couple deal with the problems faced by dual-career couples. The purpose of the present volume is to fill the clinical knowledge gap regarding the functioning of such couples.

Many, perhaps most, authors write on subjects generated in some way by their personal experiences. That is clearly the case in regard to the present work. The author himself has been in a dual-career marriage for over sixteen years. In addition, he has treated many dual-career couples over a ten-year period. Originally trained (as most therapists) in individual therapy techniques, much of the author's knowledge about marital therapy has been learned on the job. The idea for the present book was conceived out of feeling alternately perplexed and fascinated by the process and change in his own dual-career relationship, and frustrated by the lack of clinical literature to document common themes and problem areas. The task of focusing on conceptual ideas and meshing these with clinical experience has been helpful in the author's understanding of and work with dual-career couples. It is hoped that the marital therapists and couples who read this book will gain similar benefits.

Many people helped in the preparation of this volume. To each of them the author feels a special debt of gratitude. First of all, to my family, for their patience and forbearance and for their tolerance of my necessary absence from close moments and shared experiences. Next, to my colleagues, Dr. Alan Gurman and Ms. Dorothea Torstenson, for their helpful suggestions in regard to a very rough draft of the book, and for the continuing stimulation and learning produced by common interests and shared marital treatment experiences. I wish also to express appreciation to my secretary, Ms. Pat Mings, for help, often on too short notice, with typing and revising and to Ron Chambers, Senior Editor in Psychology with The Free Press, for his encouragement, enthusiasm and facilitation regarding manuscript preparation. Last, I am perhaps most indebted to the many dual-career couples I have seen in marital therapy, who have shared with me the sensitive parts of their lives. To protect confidentiality, the cases referred to in this book have been highly abstracted and somewhat fictionalized. The mutuality of our experience, however, remains very real.

·1·

Introduction

THE TWO-CAREER FAMILY represents an increasingly prevalent life-style in present-day society. From an economic standpoint, many couples are finding it necessary for both partners to be gainfully employed to reach or even to approximate their desired standard of living. Beyond financial considerations, many contemporary factors impel individuals to take advantage of their educational training and prior work experience. The change is particularly striking for women. An increasing number of married women are pursuing careers throughout the marital life cycle or returning to the labor force after an absence for parental or educational purposes.

The sociological literature uniformly suggests that the dual-career family experiences a high degree of emotional stress and strain (Bebbington, 1973; Holmstrom, 1972; and Rapoport and Rapoport, 1971). In "traditional" marriage, one spouse (usually the husband) is facilitated in the pursuit of a career by the emotional support provided and the domestic tasks performed by the other spouse (usually the wife). When both spouses have careers, role and task division usually need careful rearrangement. Flexibility and cooperation is called for in this process and spouse adaptability may be put to a severe test. At such times, and during other periods of stress, the couple may feel the need for professional help and seek marriage counseling.

Despite an accumulating literature on the sociology of the dual-career family (Paloma and Garland, 1971; Arnott, 1972; Ridley, 1972; Rapoport, Rapoport and Thiessen, 1974; Martin, Berry and Jacobsen, 1975; Rosen, Jerdee and Prestwich, 1975; Burke and Wier, 1976a; Burke and Wier, 1976b; Heckman, Bryson and Bryson, 1977; Nadelson and Eisenberg, 1977), there has been almost nothing written about the psychodynamics or psychotherapeutic treatment of dual-career couples. Berman, Sachs and Lief (1975) deal with a special instance of marital breakdown in a "two-professional" marriage. This can occur in the immediate post-training period for a couple who married during the time of their preprofessional or professional training. Relationship stress occurs as a result of differential growth and role change, usually on the wife's part, and the resultant inability of the marital relationship to adapt to these changes. However, Berman et al. do not deal with conflicts in the dual-career family over the extended marital life cycle or with marital constellations other than that represented by two professionals.

A significant and increasing number of couples are choosing to live together in a temporally extended relationship without the formal legal bonding of marriage. Many of these relationships involve two individuals who each have careers. The problems faced and the interventions utilized by a marital therapist are highly similar when a dual-career couple is living together regardless of whether they are legally married. For example, the individuals involved must cooperate so that domestic tasks can be accomplished. Likewise, the relationship parameters of influence and control need to be shared equitably, in order to promote a sense of importance and self-fulfillment for both individuals. Couples living together, but not married, have traditionally had a greater freedom to dissolve their relationship without legal interference. However, even this difference (compared to legally married couples) may be blurred as the courts come to recognize increasingly the implied contract between two people who live together, with each contributing certain resources to the relationship. For the most part, then, what is known about dual-career relationships applies to such couples living together as well as to those who are legally married.

Marital and family therapists are likely to treat individuals in dual-career relationships with increasing frequency. The psychological makeup of individuals who opt for this life-style, the particular family difficulties encountered, and the therapeutic techniques for resolving these problems are the focus of the present work. Case studies are used throughout. The emphasis is on relationships where the individuals are legally married and where both partners hold jobs for reasons other than, or in addition to, economic considerations. Also, both spouses have prepared educationally and by experience for such career-type occupations.

2

Although not the primary focus, there will be some applicability of the present material to "two-worker" families, where both spouses work, not out of felt choice, but for mainly economic purposes. Lein et al. (1974) found that the stresses faced and level of felt marital satisfaction were generally similar in dual-worker families to that found by Rapoport and Rapoport (1971) for dual-career families. However, a more recent study by Staines, Pleck, Shepard and O'Connor (1978) suggests, based on a national survey, that working wives with lower educational attainment (less than a high school diploma) report significantly lower felt marital adjustment, when compared with wives having more education.

Thus, the data is somewhat unclear in regard to whether dual-career and dual-worker families, taken as a group, suffer similar or different psychological strain. In any case, the emphasis here will be on dual-career couples, where both individuals either already hold or are preparing educationally for positions in the professional, technical or managerial areas of the occupational structure.

In the first part of the book, personality factors of individuals likely to enter dual-career marriages are explored. These are usually persons for whom achievement and recognition are important. They are willing to invest a good deal of time and energy in reaching career goals. Along these lines, they may be somewhat rigid and rather single-minded individuals at times. While often supportive of one another, they can be competitive and likely in certain instances to keep "score," leading to conflict and perceived stress.

The middle section of the book deals with problems that most frequently characterize the dual-career families who seek marriage counseling. Many of these relate to difficulties in maintaining self-esteem and the lack of felt spouse support and appreciation. As indicated previously, the emotional and/or domestic and child-care task support system likely to enhance a spouse's career in traditional (one-career) families cannot be as easily provided when both partners are employed outside the home. This can result in career-oriented spouses feeling that they are not being well "taken care of" by each other. Dependency needs are often frustrated and self-esteem is lowered. There may be a tendency to "invest" more in one's job than in the marriage, feeling the former offers a greater possibility of reward and personal gratification.

3

Career competition may then be intensified, with both partners working against one another to get what each feels is personally deserved.

The final section of the book explores therapeutic intervention with dual-career couples and elaborates helpful treatment techniques. Increasing the flexibility of available role and task behaviors and helping to change the attitudes of both spouses in certain areas is seen as both necessary and desirable. A careful exploration and revision of the marital contract (Sager, 1976) is often necessary in order to take into account the many probable changed expectations and circumstances which have occurred in the marital relationship. Freeing couples from sex-role-engendered notions of "appropriate" marital behavior is useful in this regard (Rice and Rice, 1977). Therapist suggestions for handling domestic tasks, particularly help with scheduling and managing time, can prove beneficial. Increased skill on the part of each spouse in reinforcing one another's efforts and achievements can enhance each partner's self-esteem. The use of co-therapists in treating dual-career couples is also explored and evaluated.

The reader will become quickly aware that there is no unitary guiding theory or "school" of therapy presented here for clinical work with dual-career couples. The author is fond of telling students and supervisees that he is "hopelessly eclectic" and, indeed, this is the case. The reader will find psychodynamic, intrapsychic formulations of conflict areas existing side by side with behavioral and gestalt technique recommendations for modifying such conflicts. In this manner, helping dual-career couples is very similar to actually living in this alternative marital life-style. Innovative solutions are called forth to deal with unanticipated problems and a technique that "works" is often embraced with a certain tenacity by the therapist. In this manner, over time, and across couples, certain therapeutic strategies prove effective and are retained; others prove ineffective and are dropped from one's therapeutic armamentarium.

Sharing knowledge and experience of this process with other therapists who work with dual-career couples has been enormously helpful to the author. This has provided some needed verification, on the one hand, but may have reinforced certain common values and biases, on the other. On the whole, it has been a rewarding procedure, and it is in this spirit of wanting to share information that the present volume is written. The goal is, thus, to fill an important gap in the clinical literature regarding the understanding and treatment of individuals in the increasingly common life-style represented by dual-career marriage.

·2·

Historical Perspective

THE INCIDENCE of dual-career marriage has increased sharply, particularly during the past decade. This is partly a by-product of the greatly increased number of women in the labor force. Professional women generally marry men who are also professionals (Astin, 1969; Feldman, 1973). In fact, marriage to a spouse who is not a professional man may be risky for a professional woman (Bernard, 1973). Given the socialization pattern of most contemporary women, with its caution against being the intellectual or occupational superior to one's spouse, disregarding this admonition may undermine the respect of "professional" wife for "nonprofessional" husband. This is unfortunate but, nonetheless, a reality in many such marriages. Given the above considerations, it is expected that dual-career marriages will become even more prevalent, particularly in western industrial societies (Rapoport and Rapoport, 1971).

In 1964, there were approximately 2,736,000 women in the United States, ages 25–54, employed in career-level positions (Classifications I, Professional and Technical, and II, Managerial and Administrative). By 1974, this figure had risen to approximately 4,600,000, an increase of 68% in just ten years. In 1974, it was estimated that 48.6% of these women were married, with husbands present in the home (all the above data are from Klein, 1975). This would suggest that there were approximately 2,236,000 dual-career families in the United States in 1974, with the number sharply increasing (by at least 7% a year, as estimated by extrapolation). This would place the number of 1978 dual-career families, in which the wife was between ages 25 and 54, at close to 3 million.

Across all occupational levels, the percent of working wives has increased from 40.5% in 1970 to 46.4% in 1977 (U.S. Census Bureau, *Wisconsin State Journal*, Madison, Wis., May 14, 1978).

Thus, the number of dual-worker families is much larger than the number of dual-career families. Another measure of the dramatic increase in dual-career families is shown by the fact that in 1978, 63% of families in the above-$25,000 income bracket include an employed wife, as compared with 42% in 1968 (U.S. Census Bureau, *The Capital Times,* Madison, Wis., May 16, 1978).

Despite these recent increases, the phenomenon of dual-*career* marriage as a commonly occurring life-style is of relatively recent historical vintage. Very little was written about such relationships prior to 1950. There are several reasons for the past infrequent occurrence of this type of marriage. Chief among these is the traditional pattern of mate selection and the marital role preparation of men and women during their formative years. The traditional model of marriage is efficient from the standpoint of task performance, i.e., husband and wife are assigned clearly different roles in the marriage. These tend to be highly stereotyped and, therefore, somewhat rigid in terms of prescribed behaviors. In traditional marriage, husbands are expected to perform the "instrumental" functions of providing economic support and material comforts for the family, and wives are expected to fulfill "expressive" functions by taking care of the emotional needs of husband and children and by creating a supportive and comfortable domestic environment (see Blood and Wolfe, 1960, for an elaboration of the social role dynamics in traditional marriage). This model has generally characterized the marital relationship of one's elders, parents and the majority of one's married friends. In that sense, it has been programmed into the marital aspirations and expectations of most contemporary individuals. Additional reinforcement has been provided by the media, which has usually reflected prevailing societal norms and lent support to the notion that traditional marriage indeed is "marriage" as we generally know it, at least in this country.

Given these common background socialization experiences, the adoption of a dual-career life-style involves a greater departure from social and marital role patterning for a woman than for a man. The conflicts surrounding dual-career marriage are, for the husband, less directly related to his career and more likely pertain to his domestic life. It is in the latter that a departure from his learned social-role expectations may occur. For example, he may not have been prepared for the sharing of domestic and child-care tasks, as commonly required when his wife pursues a career. On the other hand, men have been educated for and experientially directed toward a job or career; thus, the assumption of such a role within the marital framework is generally accomplished with only a small amount of personal conflict. Conflict, when it occurs for a man, is likely to be a product of the question, "What shall I do?", not "Should I do it?" A woman who pursues a career must usually deal with both of these questions, as well as a host of others. In contemporary times, she can benefit from increased social support for developing her career, as well as from an increased cohort of women in similar circumstances. Historically, however, the career woman was likely to stand essentially alone. Given this fact, it is remarkable to discover that there were viable dual-career marriages in the past, even in the limited numbers with which they occurred. The rare written historical accounts of such relationships bear testimony to the unique character of those few women in the past who sought both career and marriage.

For purposes of illustration, one such partnership will be described in some detail. This is the marriage of author Mary Wollstonecraft and philosopher William Godwin, who lived in the late eighteenth century. The knowledge of this relationship has been popularized by the women's liberation movement, whose adherents see many of the beliefs promulgated today having been ascribed to and practiced by this early feminist. Prominent in this regard was Mary's insistence upon separate working quarters, i.e., a room of her own. Thus, each partner had time and space from the other in order to pursue his or her respective occupations. Time with one another was arranged by request of one of the parties and agreement by the other. They maintained separate social lives, with each (generally) relating to his or her own coterie of friends and they appeared only occasionally at social gatherings as a couple.

A fascinating account of this relationship (Detre, 1972) notes: "The regulation of their life together was to promote 'the constancy and uninterruptedness' of both their literary pursuits. But Mary [indicates that she] is having difficulty in finding privacy and uninterrupted hours to work" (p. 80). Anticipating additional difficulties of present-day dual-career couples, the account indicates that "the domestic scene, *which was still Mary's entire responsibility,* is crowded" (p. 80, italics added). The retinue included not

8

only a nursemaid and her own young child, but also Mary's young daughter from a previous marriage.

The literary portrayal of this unusual couple suggested them to be reasonably happy, professedly in love, and united in their feelings that the traditional institution of marriage was in some ways oppressive to both men and women. Mary wrote to her husband, "I wish you, from my soul, to be riveted in my heart; but, I do not desire to have you always at my elbow" (quote from Detre, 1972, p. 79). Mary summarized her own strong beliefs in *A Vindication of the Rights of Women,* in which she stated: "If marriage be the cement of society, mankind should all be educated after the same model, or the intercourse of the sexes will never deserve the name of fellowship, nor will women ever fulfill the peculiar duties of their sex, till they become enlightened citizens, till they become free by being enabled to earn their own substance, independent of men" (quote from Detre, 1972, P. 80).

Mary Wollstonecraft's battles to further her own career in the face of the demands and expectations of traditional marriage have a familiar ring some 180 years later. Although William Godwin was supportive of her uncommon requests, it was Mary's initiative that led to most of the radical innovations in their relationship. Along these lines, Detre notes that "Godwin failed to see the inequality of this situation [Mary's uneven share of domestic responsibility] as he failed to see the illogic of his own evaluation of the female mind. While he respected and freely incorporated her ideas into the essays he was writing, he took for granted the accepted distinctions between the male and female mind." That is to say, "one [gender] is accustomed to the exercise of its reasoning powers, and the other of its feelings" (pp. 80, 81).

This historical account of the marriage of William Godwin and Mary Wollstonecraft highlights many problems commonly faced by dual-career couples today. These include: (a) balancing career and familial responsibilities; (b) attempting to provide mutual support while at the same time managing competitive feelings; (c) dealing with a finite amount of time in light of multiple role demands; and (d) preserving one's identity as a "person," as distinct from a "spouse." The preceding historical account indicates that somewhat greater personal stress is likely to be felt initially by the wife than by the husband in a dual-career marriage, as it is her behavior in pursuing a career that is deviant from

9

traditional female role expectations. It is common for the career wife to have several jobs, only one of which results in financial remuneration. In choosing to be employed outside the home, she is often adding one additional "job" to those of (a) housewife and (b) mother. Depending on the willingness of her husband to share responsibility for domestic and child-care tasks, she may have as many as three essentially full-time jobs, particularly when there is a young child or children involved. This is indeed a source of much role strain (Johnson and Johnson, 1977) for the wife, who may, in a sense, be pursuing as many as three "careers." Of course, the inevitable stress felt in such a situation by one partner is likely to have ramifications for the other, and the relationship will soon feel the strain.

Much of the stress in dual-career marriage and, indeed, in most marriages, comes from violating the couple's initial relationship contract, as formulated at the time of the marriage (Sager, 1976). Since much of this contract is implicit or subconscious, violation is inevitable. In healthy marriages, the couple is able to renegotiate their contract as the marriage grows and changes. The next chapter will focus on the marital contracts of dual-career couples and on certain aspects of how these individuals chose one another.

·3·

Marital Choice and Contract in Dual-Career Marriage

MANY OF THE SOCIOLOGICAL ASPECTS of dual-career marriage have been treated in previous writings (see especially Holmstrom, 1972, and Rapoport and Rapoport, 1971). An extended elaboration will not be undertaken here. In general, previous studies have indicated a general feeling of satisfaction with the dual-career life-style despite a high degree of perceived stress. Such couples tend to be quite busy timewise and operate on hectic schedules—at least, as far as the outside observer can tell. Friends and social life tend to be restricted and often limited in choice to other dual-career couples. In the Rapoport (1971) studies of English couples, there is commonly more than a hint of deference on the wife's part to the husband's career. This is not reported to be a source of conflict for the wife and perhaps is congruent with the greater emphasis on class and "place" that characterizes British social patterns.

Holmstrom (1972) interviewed American couples and found generally a greater degree of resentment on the wife's part toward circumstances which favored her husband's career over her own. These ranged from the (mutual) expectation that her career would be subordinated during early child rearing to feeling professionally disadvantaged because of antinepotism rules. The social and friendship patterns of the American dual-career spouses in the Holmstrom study corresponded to those found by the Rapoports for English couples. In addition, certain family background characteristics of such couples were revealed in both sets of interviews. There was often an important woman figure in the husband's and/or wife's family of origin who herself pursued a career. A discussion, in Chapter 4, of the study by Bebbington (1973) elaborates these characteristics of the families of origin for

11

dual-career couples. This chapter will focus on certain additional facets of the sociology of marriage that are helpful in understanding the psychological dynamics of dual-career relationships. Primary among these would be the question of marital choice as applied to such couples and an elaboration of their marital contract (Sager, 1976).

There are two types of dual-career marriages that can be differentiated, usually in terms of the timing of the wife's career. Some couples marry with the understanding that the wife currently has, or is preparing for, an occupation that she expects to be employed in throughout most or all of the marriage. Both partners are presumably aware of this expectancy from very early in their relationship. Their initial marital contract takes into account the fact that both spouses will have a strong temporal, intellectual, and emotional commitment to their respective jobs. This knowledge has ramifications for planning where they will live, deciding when and if they will have children, etc. Thus, the marriage structure is formed with dual-careers in mind.

The second type of common dual-career marriage pattern is one in which the wife may decide to pursue a career after the marriage has been existent for some time. The lack of felt fulfillment in her life, the fact that her children may be in school or have left home, feelings of guilt about not using her educational skills, or any number of other reasons may lead her to this decision. It may require that she go to school in order to acquire or update skills. In any case, this type of career decision usually introduces stress into the marital relationship. In part, a strain is felt because expectations about the wife's career were not likely a substantive part of the couple's initial marital contract. Revision and contract renegotiation is called for, and this necessary process can introduce a certain amount of upheaval into the marriage. The wife is likely to ask her husband for support and, usually, for help with domestic and child-care tasks. He may not be prepared for these changed expectations, feeling that his partner is asking for a different type of marital relationship than he had initially anticipated.

If the partners (especially the husband) do not have the flexibility to adapt to the changes in the marriage resulting from the wife's pursuing a career, divorce may be the eventual outcome. The wife may feel in the painful bind of having to choose between her career and her husband. Some women, unwilling to put their marriage at risk, abandon career plans at this point. This is rarely a satisfactory long-term solution, and the resultant felt frustration on the wife's part can cause stress in other aspects of the marriage. She may overinvest in her children's educational and career choices, perhaps alienating them in the process. Or she may become increasingly resentful of her husband's opportunity and implied marital relationship "permission" to pursue his career. Such feelings of hostility can block the achieving of closeness and the partners may become increasingly withdrawn from one another. A case study illustrates this process.

Case #1. Ann and Jim are in their late twenties and have been married for six years. They have a son, Tim, age 3. They entered marital therapy complaining of felt distance in their relationship and a breakdown in their ability to communicate. Jim had graduated from college and begun his own business, with startup capital provided by his family. Ann, who had completed three years of college, went to work for a social service agency two years after they were married. She had been quite successful, especially in her organizing efforts, and gained a reputation that extended beyond their small community.

Jim felt the need for additional training and decided to return to graduate school, necessitating a move to a distant city. Ann was not happy at the prospect of leaving her job. Nonetheless, she acceded to his wish and rationalized the move as being an opportunity for her to finish college and get her degree. Subconsciously, she seemed aware that Jim was feeling increasingly ambivalent about her job success, particularly in light of his own meager accomplishments with his business. She sensed some ulterior motives on his part for wanting to "get her out of town." Indeed, Jim had been surprised when Ann had gone back to work only three months after Tim was born.

Both partners came from traditional families, where the father worked and the mother stayed home to take care of the house and children. During the time they were dating, Jim and Ann had both assumed that this pattern would be repeated in their marriage. (When these expectations were discussed initially, they were just beginning to explore the idea of getting married.) Seven years later, Jim stated that he felt misled in regard to Ann's subsequent career interests by the fact that she had left college after her junior year and gone to work as a waitress in the college community. She had clearly stated her lack of interest in school and expected that she would not "go back."

Thus, Jim and Ann entered marriage with the expectation that his job would be the only outside career in the family. They did not anticipate that Ann might change her feelings in this regard. Jim was not aware early in the relationship that her changed plans would pose a threat to his own feelings of occupational competence. There had been little or no modeling in his (or Ann's) family of origin regarding the changes in a marital relationship likely to be occasioned by the wife pursuing a career.

Jim responded to Ann's involvement and obvious satisfaction from her job with increasingly suppressed anger and subsequent withdrawal. Ann felt resentment in turn at Jim's lack of support and appreciation for her efforts. Although he was willing to share housekeeping and child-care tasks, the perceived emotional alienation in the relationship outweighed these considerations. Ann began to realize increasingly that she could not feel fulfillment with the totality of her life and remain married to Jim. Although he could not yet admit it directly, it seemed obvious to the therapist that Jim had reached much the same conclusion.

By the time this couple sought professional help, the path toward divorce was well established. In essence, they appeared to be seeking confirmation from the therapist as to the "rightness" of such a decision. They also wanted to know the possible effects of a divorce on Tim. Over the course of five therapy sessions, they became more convinced that divorce was the best solution to the change in character of their marital expectations. They were reassured by the therapist's comments regarding the possible consequences of divorce on Tim, and it was obvious that they both had deep, genuine feelings for their son. They began to explore legally the possibility of a shared custody arrangement. Therapy ended shortly after Ann filed divorce papers.

The case study points out the importance of family background experiences in understanding marital choice and the initial marital contract. It is useful to focus on why individuals who opt for a dual-career marriage choose one another, especially since they are assuming a nontraditional marital life-style.

MARITAL CHOICE

The extended period of education and effort required in preparation for a career commonly involves some restriction of social life and dating behavior. One does not usually have the time and energy to meet and form extensive relationships with a variety of partners. The principle of propinquity applies to marital choice in general (Murstein, 1970). That is, an individual is more likely to choose for a partner someone who is in close geographical contact with himself or herself at the desired time of mate selection. If the choice is made relatively early in life, this means that the couple may be characterized by a high degree of homogamy, that is, basic similarity on a wide variety of background demographic and sociological variables. Studies indicate that a high degree of homogamy in a couple can generally lead to persistence of the marriage (Murstein, 1970).

There are certain, unique factors in the marital choice process for potential dual-career spouses. It is important for a career-minded individual to perceive the potential partner as also placing a high degree of importance on both partners' present or future careers. For some people, one way this reassurance can be obtained is when both individuals show strong career interests. Thus, the choice of another person with serious career intentions can serve as a validation of the importance of work in one's own life. It might also be anticipated that such an individual will understand the pressures and sacrifices required at times in the pursuit of a career, as well as the rewards and pleasures which can be derived.

Choosing a partner who affirms the centrality of work in one's life is generally adaptive for dual-career couples. The result can be synergistic, enhancing the career achievements of both spouses. This positive effect was seen in the study of sociologist husbands and wives by Martin, Berry and Jacobsen (1975). Given that men are traditionally more socially supported in their career pursuits, the degree to which such a mate choice is potentially mutually facilitative for personal and marital growth depends, in large part, on the *lack of ambivalence both partners feel toward the wife's career*. She needs to have firm career goals in mind and she needs the relatively unambivalent support of her husband. This support can be shown by a willingness to share domestic and

15

child-care responsibilities and to make personal sacrifices that will enhance her career achievement. The latter may include willingness on the husband's part to work fewer hours, spending more time at home. In some cases, support may take the form of an agreement to move to a new location that would offer *both* partners better job opportunities. Both husband and wife will need to make certain concessions regarding time and career opportunity, particularly if they wish to have children. It is important that both feel the necessary sacrifices will even out over time, particularly if there is a current feeling of unevenness in terms of what each partner is being asked to forego in order to facilitate the other's advancement.

However, the restriction of potential partners to those "close at hand," and to those also showing strong career interests, can combine to restrict one's relationship experience prior to marriage. This restriction may cause future marital difficulties. Choosing a partner who is relatively convenient may thus be only a minimal "choice" and may lead to subsequent doubts about the wisdom of having picked that individual as a mate. Future dual-career couples can place too great an emphasis on the mutual importance of work while overlooking the absence of other common interests and background similarities that could serve as potential bonding for the marriage. Carried to the extreme, this narrow focus on one aspect of the potential partners' life together can result eventually in a general constriction in the relationship. All work and no play make a dull marriage for many individuals. As a result of taking little time to develop outside social relationships, the spouses may end up feeling that they have only each other to talk to. This restriction can also limit the sources of potential self-esteem enhancement. The opinion of oneself (and of one's mate) may hinge too completely on whether the two careers are working out satisfactorily. Putting so many eggs in the career basket, so to speak, can leave both spouses feeling vulnerable to forces in the occupational world not completely under their control—e.g., the rise and fall of the stock market—if one or both partners are employed in the business world.

There are other difficulties associated with choosing a partner based primarily on similarity of career interests. Much marital restlessness, particularly that associated with the midlife crisis (Sheehy, 1976), seems to relate to the feeling of perhaps having chosen a partner prematurely, i.e., prior to having acquired enough relationship experiences with others. A particular form of dual-career marriage which illustrates this premature choice is the marrying of one's mentor. Such pairings are seen when a professor marries a graduate student, an older business executive chooses a younger executive for a partner, and so forth. Similarity of occupational interests is often a strong deciding factor in the decision of such individuals to get married. Also involved in the choice is a good deal of idealization by both partners (the younger individual admires the older, more established spouse; the older individual may recapture elements of his or her youthfulness by choosing a younger mate who is following in the same footsteps). Over time, the idealization diminishes and the two spouses must then struggle with the issue of whether there is a realistic basis for continuing their relationship.

The mentor–student type of relationship is characterized in addition by marked role fixity and often gets into difficulty when one partner attempts to break out of the defined role. The younger spouse may gain a notable degree of success on his or her own and the relationship may be unable to shift to a more egalitarian basis, in line with the comparable achievements of both individuals. Or the career directions of one or both partners may begin to diverge, generating the feeling that there is little left to hold the relationship together. The following case study illustrates some of the possible consequences when mentor marries protégé.

Case #2. Allan and Mary have been married five years and have two daughters, ages 3 years and 14 months. This is Allan's second marriage. He was married when he was 21 and divorced six years later. He has a son, Billy, age 11, who is with his ex-wife, Joan. Allan describes his first marriage as one of "honor": "Joan was pregnant and, since I thought I loved her, we decided we should get married and see if we couldn't make a go of it. We couldn't. After a while it became clear that our lives were going in pretty much different directions. She envied my success and resented being at home all the time with Billy. Eventually, the bitterness took over and we decided it was best to split and start over, maybe with someone else."

Allan, now in his thirties, is a successful artist who teaches at a small, highly-rated college, which has a limited graduate program. Mary had been one of his graduate students in the Master of Fine

17

Arts degree program. She admired Allan for his creativity and appreciated his expressed support for her fledgling artistic talents. Despite the nine years difference in their ages, Allan and Mary felt a closeness of communication and a "similarity in the way we thought about art." Mary finished her degree and the couple subsequently lived together for a year before getting married. After his experience with Joan, Allan felt that he wanted a partner who shared more common interests, that is, "someone who could understand the importance of art in my life and not be jealous of my success." Mary seemed to fit the bill.

Primarily because of Allan's age, the couple decided to have children early. As jobs were limited in the small college town, Mary had been unable to find a full-time position and ended up giving art lessons for a few hours each week. As her career commitment was lessened somewhat by the above employment circumstances, she did not protest Allan's suggestion that they have children early (and close together). Mary had observed Allan's interaction with his son, Billy, and felt he would make a good father.

Mary requested counseling for herself because of a loss of interest in sex shortly after the birth of her second daughter. After one session, the therapist, sensing that her sexual difficulties were symptomatic of problems in the marital relationship, requested that Allan also come to the sessions. Both partners agreed. It soon became clear that Mary was feeling a lack of support from Allan in regard to helping her with child care. "He seems to be interested only in his work. He'll make time for Billy but not for Jenny (their oldest daughter). I'm feeling like I'm going to have to give up my art all together, if I don't get some help."

Beneath Mary's resentment, the therapist sensed the subconscious fear that Allan's devotion to his work might lead to another relationship, this time with his current protégé. Mary's disinterest and emotional withdrawal in the sexual part of their relationship compounded her insecurity in this regard. Allan seemed aware that his (second) marriage was at risk and he seemed motivated to improve things. He sensed that a lot of the idealization had gone out of their relationship. Eventually, he was able to reassure Mary that he was not thinking of forming an intimate relationship with someone else.

After approximately ten therapy sessions, Mary began to voice strong feelings that she needed to develop her own artistic career "before it's too late." To do this meant looking for a full-time job and asking Allan for a greater time commitment in regard to domestic and child-care tasks. They agreed that such a decision would probably necessitate moving to a larger city, with its greater possibility of job opportunities, particularly for Mary. A rough period of give-and-take followed and Allan eventually acceded to starting a job search. He felt this decision represented a sacrifice on his part, since he was secure and happy in his present position.

At the end of six months (twenty therapy sessions), the couple was still looking for jobs and anticipating a move. They felt things had improved and sex was again satisfying for both partners. They decided to stop therapy at this point. The solution of moving to another city, primarily for employment reasons, felt like a necessary one to the therapist. Until plans in this regard were solidified, Allan and Mary felt a lot of ambiguity in their relationship. A phone follow-up, six months after therapy ended, indicated that they were still looking around but, because of the length of time required by the search, would be staying for another academic year. Mary said that Allan was helping her more around the house. She still felt stifled in regard to her own career plans. She volunteered that they both felt better about their relationship, however. Coming to terms with the loss of the idealization that had characterized the early part of their marriage had hopefully established the relationship on a more realistic basis. In many ways, Mary and Allan have not yet fully answered the question of whether their relationship can offer sustained mutual fulfillment.

Despite the hazards outlined above, the author's experience in treating dual-career couples suggests that an acknowledgment of the high priority of work in each spouse's value system is relatively more important psychologically in concretizing mate selection than other factors, e.g., potential economic benefits or physical attractiveness. Another important characteristic relating to mate selection has to do with the influence of modeling. Particularly for a woman, having a mother, a close woman relative, or important women friends who have had a career is helpful in her own career decision making (Bebbington, 1973; St. John-Parsons, 1978). Having close female figures in one's life who pursued a career can also be significant in a man's choosing a partner who is career minded. He may be more tolerant and encouraging of his wife's career needs, partly as a result of having observed the importance of work for the happiness and self-fulfillment of other women who have been important in his life. A case study will further illustrate the influence of these factors in mate selection.

Case #3. Fred and Sarah are in their early thirties and have been married for eight years. They have two daughters, ages 6 and 4. Fred has a successful position as a biological research scientist and Sarah is employed as a science teacher. The couple met in their first year of graduate study, dated for approximately eleven months, and subsequently were married after living together for roughly nine months. Sarah had relatively more premarital relationship experience than Fred; however, neither partner had been in a prior relationship where they had seriously considered marriage. The couple had met after being introduced by a woman friend of Sarah's, who had known Fred in high school and "thought you two would get along well together."

Fred and Sarah grew up in neighboring midwestern states—he in a suburban community and she in a medium-sized city. She had attended a smaller state college and then came to a large public university for graduate work. He had continued his graduate training at the same university where he obtained his bachelor's degree.

Fred's family consisted of a lawyer father and a mother who worked as a librarian. He had an older sister, who married shortly after finishing college and was not currently employed outside the home, and a younger sister, a dancer in a large eastern city. Fred's mother had worked prior to the birth of his older sister and then had resumed her career when his younger sister was 3 years old. He generally spoke warmly of his family but perceived his father to be somewhat distant and overinvolved in his work. Fred remembers the family as taking only a few vacations together during the time he was growing up. His mother had stimulated Fred's curiosity about the world, often bringing home interesting books from the library for him to read, particularly in scientific areas.

Fred's childhood and adolescence were generally uneventful, except that he blamed a moderately severe case of acne for his limited dating experience in high school. He generally presents himself as having been quite serious-minded, with little of the "play" or other expression of adolescent rebellious feelings that likely characterized his peers. Fred remembers, somewhat enviously, his older sister's popularity and greater social ease, and he noted that the latter quality also characterized his father's personality.

Sarah's family background was punctuated by her parents' divorce when she was 12. Somewhat surprisingly, she is still unclear as to the precipitants of this, but has the vague impression that her father (a small businessman) had been involved with another woman. Her father had remarried when she was sixteen, to a woman "not unlike my mother." Sarah has a brother, two years younger, who is a career officer in the navy. Her mother has not remarried and the memories of her mother's loneliness and pain during her teen years are still poignant. In addition, she remembers her mother's financial dependency (in the form of alimony and child support) as a source of stress and apprehension in their life. On more than one occasion, it was necessary for her mother to threaten legal action when her father was in arrears with the support payments. Sarah had worked after school and on weekends during high school and this had restricted her social life to some degree. She remembers feeling uncomfortable about questions from her peers concerning her (divorced) parents, and at times felt envious that her friends' parents were still living together.

A significant figure in Sarah's background was a married aunt (her mother's sister) who lived in the same town and was employed as a public health nurse. Sarah was fond of her aunt and admired her dedication to her job and the sense of worthwhileness derived from it. Her aunt and uncle did not have children of their own and, because of this, often treated Sarah like a "daughter."

During their respective college years both Fred and Sarah were serious students, who generally would forego social events if there was a conflict with academic demands. Fred, slowly getting over his skin problems, gradually began to date more frequently than he had in high school. Sarah, by contrast, led a somewhat monastic existence in which she deeply and enthusiastically pursued her studies. She dated during high school, but had not formed any serious relationships during that time. She continued to work part time throughout her college years, in order to "help

21

Mom out." She remembers college as a "happy" period, and does not feel deprived in regard to her limited social experience, feeling she chose willingly to "emphasize books over boys."

When asked what attracted them to one another, Sarah said "we seemed to be interested in the same things," and "I liked the way he (Fred) was thoughtful about different things." Fred also indicated that common interests were important but said, in addition, "she (Sarah) seemed to appreciate the way I was, and didn't try to change me into someone else." When asked what was salient in their decision to get married, Fred said in a rather matter-of-fact manner, "I felt it was about time to get married." Sarah more or less agreed.

After getting her master's degree at the end of her second year of graduate work, Sarah worked for three years until Fred obtained his doctorate. Then they moved to their present location, after Fred was offered a job there. Sarah said the location had been determined primarily by Fred's job offer but said she "wouldn't have gone unless I was sure there would be job opportunities for me." As it turned out, Sarah was unable to find a teaching job during their first year in the present location. Toward the middle of that year, she became pregnant and several months thereafter received a teaching job offer for the following fall, which would start only a short time after her due date. With relatively little apparent ambivalence, she accepted the job and later arranged for child care. Fred indicated that the choice to go back to work soon after the baby's anticipated arrival was "left up to Sarah." He stated: "We could have managed (financially) if she had wanted to stay home. But her going back didn't surprise me. She's much happier working."

Subsequent to the birth of their oldest daughter, Fred has helped with the child care, although the major responsibility has remained Sarah's and this was particularly the case during the early years of child rearing. Sarah notes that "Fred got more interested in the children once they became 'people,' if you know what I mean. He doesn't quite know what to do with them when they are little and helpless, but once they started talking in conversation, he got more turned on." Fred nodded his agreement with Sarah's assessment, adding that he was looking forward to his oldest daughter learning how to read more fluently.

With other domestic responsibilities, Fred has shown a willingness to share in the household tasks, and this has been particularly true during the times Sarah has worked (she spends each summer at home). Neither spouse reports a felt inequity in this regard, although Sarah spends more time doing domestic chores than Fred. They generally do different tasks, but both seem satisfied with this aspect of their relationship.

They entered marital therapy in late summer of their eighth year of marriage, largely upon Sarah's initiative. She stated: "We're drifting apart. I know I'm holding back and I don't know why. I don't feel as close to Fred as before and there's definitely less intimacy now." Further questioning indicated that, during the spring of the preceding school year, she had begun to have strong feelings and sexual fantasies toward a male teacher at her school. Neither Fred nor Sarah had prior or subsequent extramarital sexual relationships. She had felt guilty and conflicted about these feelings and, prior to therapy, had not shared them directly with Fred, although she professed: "I felt many times I should tell him. But I didn't know how he would feel about it or how he'd take it." The coming of summer had partly solved the conflict, but she began to grow more anxious as the upcoming school year rapidly approached.

They described their sexual relationship during marriage as generally "okay," although Sarah had noted a diminution of interest on her part following the birth of their second child: "I guess I was just tired." This lasted for about a year, and then things "went back to normal." Fred expressed a general satisfaction with their life and seemed partly surprised at Sarah's disclosure of her fantasied involvement with another man. However, he seemed to rationalize this by saying, "Well, I've been attracted to other women at the Lab, but I've never done anything about it." He had sensed some loss of intimacy in the relationship, but was not as troubled by this as Sarah. Fred stated: "I know from talking to other people that this happens. But I could see it was really bothering her and I thought we better come in (to therapy) and talk about it. I don't want a divorce." The latter statement was somewhat perplexing to the therapist, in that neither party had brought up the idea of separation and/or divorce as a solution to their current problems.

The couple was seen in short-term marital therapy for a total of fourteen sessions over a six-and-one-half-month period. As a guide in assessing marital difficulties and in formulating therapeutic strategies, the author has found it useful to help the couple reconstruct some idea of their initial marital contract, i.e., the expectations, hopes, and wishes of each spouse for themselves and for the relationship in the early stages (Sager et al., 1971; Sager, 1976). A formulation of Fred and Sarah's marital contract is presented in Table 1. Both the initial contract and those revisions that took place during the period of marital therapy are presented.

THE MARITAL CONTRACT

For dual-career couples, focusing on the initial contract is particularly helpful for determining the spouses' early expectations in regard to their respective careers. As Sager has indicated, there are conscious, verbalized expectations, as well as preconscious and unconscious expectations that govern relationship behaviors. The latter operate out of awareness and are not verbalized by the couple. It is the unconscious, nonverbalized expectations that have the greatest potential for causing marital difficulty. This results in part from the fact that unconscious aspects of the marital contract may be inherently contradictory and often have strong determinants from experiences in one's family of origin. An example would be strong, unresolved sexual feelings toward a parent that the individual was first aware of during adolescence. Such feelings may have been aroused and prolonged by the parent's seductive behavior. The conflictual feelings engendered may have been suppressed by the individual during premarital sexual relationships. The onset of marriage, with its inevitable re-creation of certain aspects of one's family of origin, may have led to a resurfacing of such sexual conflicts. The result of this intrapsychic process can be a sexual inhibitedness that causes problems for the couple. The individual may not make the connection between present sexual difficulties and prior familial conflicts. In this example, the marital contract may contain contradictory clauses. The husband may feel: "You are my wife and I want an intense sexual experience with you." At the same time, unconsciously, he may react: "When I've had these intense sexual feelings before, in my family, I've known they are not right and I can't let myself express them." In this sense, conflicts from

24

one's family of origin (or other prior interpersonal relationships) represent a sort of excess baggage brought into the marriage from the past that, nonetheless, can exert a powerful effect on the relationship.

Table 1. Aspects of Fred and Sarah's marital contract—initial and revised (during and after therapy) formulations.

A. INITIAL CONTRACT

Sarah	*Fred*
CONSCIOUS (VERBALIZED) ASPECTS	CONSCIOUS (VERBALIZED) ASPECTS
I need my career for a variety of reasons and expect your support.	I respect your right to a career and appreciate its importance for your sense of satisfaction and well-being. I saw this as true for my mother and that's why I can understand it.
I'm willing to support your career, including taking care of home and children, in return for your acknowledgment of my need to work at a meaningful job.	I appreciate your willingness to support my career, as it is important for me to feel a sense of achievement there. I'll help out at home as much as I can.
I am aware of your respect for me as a person, and I will try to accept you for who you are.	It is important for you to accept me as I am, as I have not always felt acceptable to a woman.
UNCONSCIOUS (NONVERBALIZED) ASPECTS	UNCONSCIOUS (NONVERBALIZED) ASPECTS
Because I need my career, I'm willing to take on three jobs. I'll do the housework and take care of any children. I don't really expect you'll make this any easier for me. After all, my mother didn't get much help.	My career is really more important than yours. Therefore, I want you to take care of the home (and any children we have) so I can be free to work.
One reason I must work is that I cannot let myself feel the pain and vulnerability my mother did, because she could not support the family materially after her divorce. I'd rather be like my aunt, who could take care of herself.	I have heard you speak about the distress of your family after the divorce, and I will try to understand and accept this, but I don't really know what it means for us.

It is important that we have a happy marriage, because I do not want to get a divorce like my parents.

I am afraid to get too close to you because then you could leave me and hurt me like my father did my mother.

It is important that we have a happy marriage because it was painful to feel so alone when I was a teenager.

I'm afraid to get too close to you because you will find something to criticize in me and then you will leave me.

B. REVISED CONTRACT

Sarah

CONSCIOUS (VERBALIZED) ASPECTS

I understand that it is a fear of rejection that has caused me to hold back, and it now feels safer to get a little closer.

I will probably have sexual fantasies toward other people, but I feel less fear of them or need to act on them.

My career is still very important to me and it is necessary to separate this from my feelings about Robert (the other teacher).

UNCONSCIOUS (NONVERBALIZED) ASPECTS

My career is vital to my well-being, but I don't know if I can put it above my marriage and my children.

Although I can let myself get closer to you, I still feel afraid that you will leave me if I don't make you happy. I think that another teacher could understand my work and help me do a better job.

Fred

CONSCIOUS (VERBALIZED) ASPECTS

I understand that it is a fear of rejection that has caused me to hold back, and it now feels safer to get a little closer.

I will continue to have sexual fantasies toward other people, but I'm pretty sure I won't act them out.

I know I can make such a separation, since I have done it in my own relationships. I reaffirm that your career is important and I will continue to support you in it.

UNCONSCIOUS (NONVERBALIZED) ASPECTS

My career is more important than Sarah's. That is why it is right for her to do more around the house and to take care of the children more than I do.

I do not know that you won't pull away from me again and prefer another man; therefore, I am unsure how close to really let myself get to you.

26

It is important for a marriage to be able to grow and change as the partners themselves change. Thus, the marital contract usually needs to undergo periodic revision over the course of the marriage. Most couples do this contract revision themselves, without feeling the need for therapeutic intervention. Marital contract revision, however, is usually both an important marital therapy task and a criterion against which to assess the effects of therapy. As Sager notes, not all aspects of the contract will be revised with time and experience; certain unconscious aspects may remain more or less the same without causing undue present or future marital disruption.

In Sarah and Fred's case, Table 1 indicates that the unconscious or nonverbalized fear that Sarah might end up divorced and unable to take care of herself in part motivated her toward career achievement and, at the same time, set limits on the degree of intimacy she could comfortably attain in her marriage. Sarah's holding back did not ostensibly trouble Fred to the degree one might expect. This can be partly understood as the by-product of his own fears of rejection, which become aroused if he gets too involved in a relationship with a woman. The outcome of this intimacy-limiting process was periodic difficulty with commitment to the marriage on the part of both partners (Salzman, 1973). As a by-product of these underlying mutual fears, their marriage was generally characterized by a rather passive congeniality (Cuber and Haroff, 1966), and by an implicit agreement not to make each other uncomfortable by placing too great a demand for closeness. These expectations are consistent with both Fred's and Sarah's limited involvement in serious relationships with other people prior to their marriage. Each had rationalized this; Fred blamed his skin problems and Sarah felt the seriousness of work and study demands precluded an intense involvement with another person. Developmentally, this lack of prior experience put a lot of pressure on the marital relationship. It was easy to expect that marriage would satisfy all or, certainly, most of each partner's interpersonal needs. This expectation was still somewhat idealized, having never been tempered by the reality of what deep prior relationships had and had not been able to provide in terms of personal need gratification. Although mutually disappointed with the degree of intimacy in their marriage, they, to a certain extent, lacked a baseline of comparison, since there were few prior relationships. In the early phases of their relationship, Fred and

27

Sarah appear to have both "backed off" and worked out their implicit agreement to limit the mutual demands for intimacy.

Had Sarah's fantasies of having a more intense relationship (with another man) not come to the fore, this couple might not have felt the need for therapy. The fantasied relationship could well represent Sarah's unconscious identification with her father and thus could arouse the ambivalence she felt toward him for leaving her mother for another woman. The fantasied "affair" might also have been a way of indirectly showing her anger toward Fred for certain inequities in the marriage, e.g., her disproportionate share of domestic and household tasks. She denied having any overt hostile feelings in this regard.

In the future, one might expect Sarah increasingly to feel less grateful to Fred for "letting her have" a career and to experience greater resentment over her inequitable share of domestic and child-care responsibilities. If she becomes bitter over the fact that she has done this to help him "get ahead" at the expense of her own career achievement, competitive feelings are likely to be aroused. When and if this happens, Sarah may again pull back in the relationship, showing the pattern of anger blocking intimacy frequently seen in couples who seek marital therapy. A six-month phone follow-up after therapy ended suggested that things were generally going well for the couple.

The case of Fred and Sarah also illustrates the importance of modeling in one's career aspirations and felt acceptance by others. Fred's understanding, tolerance, and verbal, albeit limited temporal, support for Sarah's career seemed partly the result of his mother's having worked outside the home for a substantial part of his growing-up period. He had a real sense of the meaning and importance of work in the lives of *both* men and women. Sarah's identification with an aunt and this woman's career was likewise important from a modeling standpoint. It also served to illustrate that having a career might also serve as a potential "escape route" for Sarah, should her marriage not work out. In other words, it was a partial guarantee that she would never have to suffer the pain and humiliation endured by her mother, who was unable to support the family materially after her father left.

Therapy was helpful to Fred and Sarah partly in terms of pointing out how experiences in their families and personal traumas while growing up were carried over into their marital interaction, contributing to their difficulties with emotional and sexual intimacy. Career-related conflicts were not particularly salient at the time but could be a source of potential difficulty for this couple, as noted above.

In summary, the area of dual-career couples' marital choice has been explored and several case studies presented. An affirmation of the importance of work and career achievement for *both* partners is viewed as a critical aspect in marital choice. Modeling of such ideas and supportive behaviors in one's family of origin or from other important figures in one's life is seen as often useful. Pertinent aspects of marital choice and the marital contract of one dual-career couple seen in therapy were presented, along with revised aspects of the contract that occurred during and after therapy.

·4·

Personality Interaction Patterns of Dual-Career Spouses

A CRITICAL FACTOR in understanding and treating dual-career marriages is an appreciation of the personality patterns which characterize individuals likely to adopt this life-style. Although there are exceptions, each spouse in a dual-career marriage generally places a high premium on achievement. They commonly expect and have usually experienced success in many endeavors, expect this to continue, and tend to be self-critical in situations where they perceive their efforts to have fallen short. Circumstances and events which facilitate the achievement of success are desired and appreciated while those which impede progress in this regard are sources of frustration and self-denigration.

Previously, it was noted that "traditional" marriage is oriented toward promoting occupational achievement on the part of the husband, in part via the creation of a facilitative emotional and domestic support structure. The wife in a traditional relationship is expected to make certain personal sacrifices necessary for enhancing her husband's career. She must often put aside career and other aspirations of her own, agree to settle geographically where his job is located, and attempt to adjust her life-style to the demands of and the rewards provided by his occupation. He, in turn, works hard to provide economic security and material benefits for his family. The husband's occupational success can provide a vicarious sense of advancement for his wife. This may, in part, satisfy her own suppressed desires for achievement and may reinforce the value of personal sacrifices in order to provide her husband with a supportive structure in the relationship.

In a dual-career marriage, the wife is not usually willing or desirous of suppressing her own wishes and needs for occupational achievement. She is likely to feel dissatisfaction with a life-style which confines her opportunities for personal advancement to home and family. She may feel guilty for not maximizing her educational attainments through continued work and career. In a dual-career marriage, husband and wife expect *mutual* support and reinforcement for their occupational efforts and successes.

Ideally, the presence of similar needs and values should provide a basis for empathic understanding of one another's strivings. Too often the similarity of desires becomes a source of conflict. Both spouses may feel that they are competing for a limited amount of relationship support in their individual efforts toward personal growth and accomplishment. The physical and emotional effort expended in their careers can leave both partners exhausted. At such moments, both spouses may feel the need for nurturance and support, but neither partner is in a position to provide this. The simultaneous occurrence of stress in their lives can also work against the mutual provision of support. If both are working hard toward a promotion, or if they are feeling conflict with their respective superiors, it may be difficult to come through emotionally for one another. The line between empathic understanding and concern for a commonly experienced situation, on the one hand, and felt competition and alienation, on the other, may be thin indeed. Unless such times are balanced in the relationship by occasions where each can support the other during a stressful period, one partner may feel he or she is not getting a fair emotional share from the marriage. Over time, this perceived inequity builds up resentment and can lead to marital conflict.

MARITAL CONFLICT IN DUAL-CAREER COUPLES

Earlier studies indicated a remarkable tendency of dual-career spouses to deny marital conflict, particularly that stemming from feelings of competitiveness (Holmstrom, 1972; Rapoport and Rapoport, 1971). For example, 13 of 20 couples in the Holmstrom study reported an absence of competitive feelings about their respective careers. This denial of felt competitiveness is even more surprising in the light of an almost universal agreement by previous writers that dual-career marriage represents a high-stress life-style (Berman, Sacks and Lief, 1975; Burke and Weir, 1976a; Johnson and Johnson, 1977; St. John-Parsons; 1978).

Bebbington (1973) studied 14 dual-career couples in England and concluded: "The many sources of strain are one of the most pronounced features of the dual-career family" (p. 533). He focused on developmental experiences, particularly for the wives, that could explain their choice of a potentially stressful marital arrangement. In line with the previously indicated greater social role "deviance" for wives in such marriages (see Chapter 2), husbands in dual-career marriages did not differ essentially from husbands in a "traditional" marriage control group in regard to background and predisposing factors. Therefore, personality factors of the dual-career wives were the focus of the Bebbington study.

Among the features which appeared frequently in this group of women were: (a) tendency to be the oldest or only child (50%, compared with roughly 24% of the "traditional" marriage control group sample); (b) no other adults, besides parents, in the home during childhood and adolescence; (c) employed and occupationally oriented mother (50%, compared with 20% of control group wives); Holmstrom (1972) also indicates 50% of women in her sample had mothers with extensive work histories; (d) tense relationship with their father (only 14% of the dual-career wives reported *little* tension in the family during their childhood); and (e) either prolonged separation or other potentially psychologically unsettling experiences when growing up.

Bebbington concludes that the choice of a highly stressful life-style is consistent with these women having learned to adapt to a greater than usual degree of tension and stress-producing conditions during childhood and adolescence. Similar background characteristics for dual-career wives are reported by St. John-Parsons (1978), who also found dual-career wives were generally from higher socioeconomic backgrounds than their husbands. However, the use of a small sample (N = 10) limits the generalizability of the St. John-Parsons findings. The role of modeling (having an important woman figure in one's life who had a career), previously discussed (see Chapter 3), is also borne out in the Bebbington study. Although samples are small, the data presented by Bebbington (1973) and St. John-Parsons (1978) offer a fascinating and somewhat unique look (among other writings) at the background experiences of dual-career wives.

Unfortunately, the couples studied by Bebbington may not be generally representative of dual-career couples in certain important aspects. For example, all these couples were "at a plateau stage in their development; both career and family firmly established and role changes less frequent" (p. 534). Such older, more established dual-career couples may represent a sample bias in the direction of those dyads who have adapted well to stress. The dual-career spouses interviewed by Rapoport and Rapoport (1971), by Holmstrom (1972), and by St. John-Parsons (1978) similarly represent "well established" groups. While these studies may provide a normative base for understanding functional dual-career marital relationships, they offer only limited insight into the sources of psychological problems and conflicts in such individuals.

Younger dual-career couples are somewhat more likely to feel stress and strain in their relationships without being able to employ tried-and-true coping behaviors. In a study of 196 couples where both spouses were psychologists, Bryson, Bryson and Johnson (1978) found younger couples reporting a greater degree of marital dissatisfaction. This was particularly true for the wives, especially where the couple had children. The wife was expected to take a greater amount of responsibility for child care, and this was often at the expense of her career advancement. Older couples seemed more accepting of the differential career patterning for husband and wife. Staines et al. (1978) report a similar heightened felt dissatisfaction for wives in dual-career marriages in which there were young children.

Given the high degree of stress inherent in dual-career marriage, it is important to gain a greater understanding of the genesis of psychological conflicts in such couples. Not surprisingly, marriage counselors are beginning to see such couples with increasing frequency. Data are not yet available to document whether dual-career couples appear for counseling in greater numbers than their proportional representation among married dyads. However, younger dual-career couples, who feel less secure in and not as temporally committed to their marriages, are increasingly looking for psychological help.

Berman et al. (1977) found larger than expected numbers of couples in the 27–32 age range requesting counseling. They had been married on the average for seven years and thus represented the popularized "seven-year itch" syndrome. Berman et al. did not state the proportion of their sample couples in dual-career relationships. However, their clinical case examples were about such individuals. The author's own experience of working in an urban outpatient clinic setting suggests a relatively high proportion of dual-career couples in this age range seek professional help for felt marital problems.

Berman et al. relate the disproportionate number of help-seeking couples from this age grouping to the frequent questioning of values, career and spouse choice and general life-style stresses that accompany the passage from the twenties to the thirties. This life review can be a source of psychological difficulty, particularly for individuals who may not yet feel a solid commitment to one another. Dual-career individuals may have special difficulty in making such commitments, in part because of anxiety surrounding the possibility that they might fail in such an important endeavor. This difficulty can be understood as a by-product of the personality pattern dynamics which typify spouses in this type of marital relationship. There are three prominent personality characteristics or themes commonly found in partners who adopt a dual-career life-style: (a) need for achievement, (b) strong narcissistic and/or self-esteem enhancement needs, and (c) difficulties in forming a sustained interpersonal commitment. These are discussed below.

NEED FOR ACHIEVEMENT

Dual-career spouses typically *both* desire, and are accustomed to attaining, relatively high levels of achievement. Barnett (1971) elaborates a helpful conceptual framework for understanding the psychological dynamics of high achievement–oriented persons. Professional individuals, who represent the most researched group of dual-career spouses, commonly show many behaviors (e.g., conscientiousness, perseverance, preference for organization) consistent with high need for achievement. The fact that they are generally successful people, by definition, can lead to the reinforced fixity and persistence of such behaviors with relatively little expressed anxiety or other overt manifestations of neurotic conflict. Many of these behaviors are generally facilitative for both spouses and not debilitating to the marriage. For example, both partners may actively collaborate to provide a support structure which will facilitate each other's achievement.

Martin, Berry and Jacobsen (1975) elaborate one facilitative aspect of dual-career marriage in their study of husband and wife sociologists. One partner (usually the husband) had information and experience helpful to his spouse for successfully negotiating the academic "ladder." Usually, this was shared freely within the relationship. The adaptive aspects of mutual high achievement needs may, in part, explain the surprising absence of prior writings concerning psychological dysfunction in dual-career couples. As long as these personality traits are mutually facilitative, little evidence of personal or marital psychological breakdown requiring professional intervention is likely to be manifested.

Barnett, however, points out certain underlying areas of potential conflict (particularly, in regard to dependency and the need for narcissistic or self-esteem gratification) for such individuals. When both spouses show these personality characteristics, the potential for felt psychological difficulties is likely to be increased. The majority of the case studies presented in this volume illustrate attempts by dual-career couples to arrange a functional marital system that will promote the achievement of *both* spouses, without too great a cost to the marital relationship.

SELF-ESTEEM NEEDS

Barnett notes that a prominent basic need of high-achievement individuals is for reliable narcissistic, self-esteem-enhancing gratifications. This can be expressed in terms of needing frequent "strokes" and signs of appreciation for one's efforts. Much of the energy expended toward achievement by such individuals may be in the service of receiving the accolades and acknowledgments of others. The prototype of this is in the child's performance of certain behaviors (e.g., talking, expressing affection) to gain parental attention and reward. Introjected aspects of the parent's response become the basis for feelings of self-esteem. Over time, the parent responds to certain behaviors (e.g., fighting with sibs, "talking back") with displeasure. Parental disapproval can lead to introjected negative feelings and lowered self-esteem.

The adult counterpart of the above process occurs when an individual grants other people (e.g., one's spouse, the boss, friends) a great deal of power to affect feelings of self-worth. If one's efforts are not rewarded and appreciated by others, there can be subsequent felt self-esteem injury. The more one develops an intimate relationship with another person, the greater the possibility for such injury (and, likewise, the higher the valuing of positive "strokes"). Thus, marriage has a high potential both for inflicting narcissistic injury and for boosting self-esteem.

The strong need for self-esteem enhancement likely to be felt by both spouses in a dual-career marriage makes this area a particular source of marital conflict. A partner inattentive to one's ego needs will be perceived by the other as being insensitive and uncaring. A typical response in this situation is for the "wounded" spouse to withdraw as a means of self-protection. The withdrawal, in turn, frustrates mutual dependency needs, and a vicious cycle begins. Barnett indicates that such individuals are likely to use dependency-seeking behaviors in the service of narcissistic gratification. Thus, a spouse will feel loved (and esteemed) to the extent that he or she feels "taken care of" by the partner. Withdrawal of caretaking is painful because it is felt as a narcissistic injury. In dual-career marriages, withdrawal often takes the form of withholding support for one's spouse or behaving in ways which interfere with the couple's carefully balanced emotional and domestic support system. In this regard, several studies have pointed out that a high level of spouse support is critical for the successful functioning of dual-career families (Bailyn, 1970; Holmstrom, 1972; Rapoport and Rapoport, 1971). Withdrawal of support by one partner as a response to felt frustration can thus be quite disruptive to a dual-career relationship or, indeed, to any form of marriage. A case study illustrates these dynamic processes:

Case #4. John and Susan are in their late twenties. They have been married for six years and have no children. John has recently begun a professional job and Susan has been employed in a career-level civil service position for five years, providing the financial resources for the couple during John's professional training. Susan recently completed her master's degree and expects this will enhance the opportunity for advancement in her job. At times, she entertains the option of working fewer hours and "taking it easy," letting John's income provide the majority of their financial needs. He does not yet feel established occupationally and has encouraged her to continue working full time. She is somewhat resentful of this and feels that this behavior does not conform to their (largely unspoken) initial marital contract expectations of *mutual* support and dependency. Since Susan feels she "took care of" John during the emotionally and temporally demanding years of his training, she now expects him to do the same for her. When he puts in long hours at the job, with little time and energy left over for the marital relationship, Susan feels "ripped off." She has a sense of continually having to put the marriage on "hold," always waiting for John to achieve this or that, so that he can feel secure and be more emotionally available for their relationship.

Although in some ways Susan would like to put more effort into advancing her career, she feels currently the lack of an emotional support base in the marriage for her to do this. John gives her the impression that he is more interested in her paycheck than in her career success and satisfaction. Consequently, Susan has begun to talk about cutting back to half time and having a baby. John says that he would prefer to wait and have a family when he is more established. She can acknowledge that she may wish to turn to a child for some of the emotional gratification that is missing currently in the marital relationship, due partly to his withdrawal into his work. She is pessimistic that John will share equitably in caring for a child and thus feels that she must make a career sacrifice in order to have a family. Since she likes her work and has received a good deal of praise for her efforts, she feels that decreasing the amount of time she spends at work could create a void in her life. It might also feel like a negation of the time and effort she spent getting her master's degree. She is at a critical choice point and is ambivalent about the possibility of advancement in her job versus taking on the responsibilities of parenthood. She expresses the wish for someone to talk to about these decisions and is unhappy with the current lack of communication with John in this regard.

This couple illustrates the many tradeoffs necessary to make a dual-career relationship (or any marital relationship) workable and satisfying. The case study illustrates the need for mutual self-esteem enhancement and the monitoring of dependency gratification (how well each feels taken care of by the other) as an indicator of the degree to which one's spouse fulfills these needs. John and Susan both need a sense of appreciation for their efforts. They are willing to make certain sacrifices and to take care of one another in proportion to the degree of acknowledgment for such efforts. When they married there were largely unspoken expectations that support, appreciation and caretaking by one spouse or the other would even up over time. *Each* spouse wanted respect from the other for his or her career aspirations. They did not realistically anticipate the difficulty of balancing the emotional demands of marriage with the time and energy requirements of their careers. At this point, both John and Susan have withdrawn to a certain degree their emotional investment from the marital relationship. He has escaped into his work and she into the fantasy of having a child. In this manner, they may become more like couples in a traditional marriage, and less like those with a dual-career life-style. John's ambivalence toward Susan's career has increased as he has become more involved in his own work and more financially independent of Susan. A critical element for perceived satisfaction in a dual-career marriage, i.e., spouse support, is not currently present for Susan. She is unhappy about this and her commitment to her career is wavering. If she works half time and/or has a child, it may well set the marriage on a more traditional course. Any moves away from a dual-career life-style which require Susan to make compromises in her career direction could have negative, "ripple" effects for her future happiness and sense of well-being. These feelings would undoubtedly carry over into the marriage and result in future problems for the couple.

DILEMMA OF INTERPERSONAL COMMITMENT

A further source of difficulty for couples characterized by mutual high-achievement needs may be the difficulty of making a true commitment in their interpersonal relationships (Salzman, 1973). Part of the emphasis on achievement in such individuals can be understood as a wish to avoid experiencing failure. In addition, the desire for perfection commonly accompanies high needs for achievement. School and work offer tangible indications of success, in the form of grades, promotions, salary increases, etc. But interpersonal relationship accomplishments are likely to be perceived somewhat more subjectively. This perception reflects, to some extent, the ambiguities and inconsistencies inherent in all relationships, and the inevitable mixture of feelings one has when attempting a unitary assessment of a complex phenomenon.

Couples often sense that certain relationship problems may not have concrete solutions, e.g., the difficulty in balancing occupational and marital time and emotional commitments so that one does not feel pulled in several directions at once. Moreover, there are few "guarantees" in marriage and few explicit guidelines as to how to "make it work." This is particularly true in dual-career marriage, which represents an emerging life-style, with few models of such a relationship likely to be available to the spouses. Even if one's parents both had careers, the relationship outside of work is likely to have been rather traditional. In this sense, the wife had two jobs (work and home), or three (if there were children), compared to the husband's one (Bernard, 1972).

All of the above uncertainties of the dual-career marital lifestyle increase the anticipation that one might "fail" in marriage and should, therefore, be cautious about committing oneself. Moreover, if one partner feels a greater degree of commitment to the relationship than is perceived to be present in one's spouse, feelings of vulnerability can result. The more committed spouse may then withdraw to a more distant but comfortable emotional level. The less committed spouse will subsequently feel the partner's distance and be perplexed by it. All these song-and-dance maneuvers tend to delay married individuals' being able to sense a true commitment to the relationship. In dual-career marriage, turning to work and away from the relationship is a common result of the felt vulnerability in regard to a perceived lack of spouse commitment. When this happens, there may be less motivation to put in the effort required for the restoration of emotional intimacy, as each spouse is protecting against felt rejection and a sense of personal failure in the relationship.

Thus, dual-career couples often take a long time before making a true commitment to their relationship. The possibility afforded by their careers of being financially independent and able to make it on their own can work against an early strong commitment to the marriage. Both individuals may hedge their bets and avoid working on the relationship by placing greater emphasis and effort on their careers (Holmstrom, 1972). As the previous example with Susan and John illustrates, this can take its toll over time, with one or both partners feeling an emotional void in the relationship. On the other hand, once the spouses feel able to

39

make a commitment, they are inclined to work hard at the relationship in order to perceive ultimately that they have achieved a successful marriage (Rapoport and Rapoport, 1971).

THE CONCEPT OF EQUITY

The case of Susan and John illustrates a strong motivating force that is operative in many dual-career marriages, namely, the expectation of equity (Rapoport and Rapoport, 1975; Hopkins and White, 1978; Walster, Walster and Berscheid, 1978). Over time and across situations, each partner needs to be able to anticipate and perceive that the relationship "balances out" evenly. Effort is expended and reward given with this principle in mind. One makes sacrifices (e.g., Susan worked to help put John through school) based on the expectation that the spouse will ultimately make this up to the partner. The mode of payback can vary, and does not necessarily imply a like-for-like correspondence. Thus, in the example, Susan did not expect that John would support her while she went back for further graduate training, as she had done for him, although she did anticipate that his financial earnings during this period would make it easier for the couple. She also expected his help and support in other ways—e.g., by sharing domestic responsibilities—which would enable her to feel that John was participating equitably in the relationship.

Walster, Walster and Berscheid (1978) provide a useful formulation of the concept of equity and summarize the accumulating empirical evidence in this regard. They state three (among other) propositions useful in understanding the behavior of dual-career couples:

Proposition I. Individuals will try to maximize their outcomes (where outcomes equals rewards minus costs).

Proposition II. [This proposition has to do with perceived equity in groups and thus is not as pertinent to dual-career couples as the other propositions.]

Proposition III. When individuals find themselves participating in inequitable relationships, they will become distressed. The more inequitable the relationship, the more distress individuals will feel.

Proposition IV. Individuals who discover they are in an inequitable relationship will attempt to eliminate their distress by restoring equity. The greater the inequity that exists, the more distress they will feel, and the harder they will try to restore equity. (Walster, Walster and Berscheid, 1978, p. 6)

In regard to Proposition IV, Walster et al. suggest that a person can restore either *actual* equity (by altering one's own or one's partner's relative gains from the relationship) or restore *psychological* equity (by distorting reality, e.g., trying to convince oneself that a perceived inequitable relationship is, in fact, equitable). The concept of psychological equity may well explain the denial used by many dual-career couples to handle situations of perceived inequity (e.g., the uneven responsibility for child care commonly assumed by the wife).

Walster et al. note the difficulty and subjectivity involved in assessing equity/inequity within intimate relationships. Yet such assessments do occur and result in strong positive and/or negative feelings. Because of the psychological defensiveness aroused, it is often hard for the individual or couple to admit felt inequities in the relationship. Therefore, they are frequently puzzled in regard to the source of strong negative feelings and do not often relate such feelings directly to a perception of things being unfair. However, when a sense of perceived inequity as the basis for such feelings is so labeled by a person outside the system (e.g., a therapist), they are more likely to be acknowledged and even readily accepted as relating to marital conflict.

The concept of equity transcends in a more pragmatic manner that of egalitarianism, and introduces a sense of fairness rather than equality as the essential component for evaluating aspects of the relationship. Marital partners do not usually expect each other to be equal in all facets of their life or require equal participation in every activity. Indeed, trying to vacuum the floor with each spouse having one hand on the vacuum cleaner can be quite inefficient, although it does epitomize "togetherness." Equity is also differentiated from notions of reciprocity, or *quid pro quo* (Lederer and Jackson, 1968) which imply each action by one spouse must be met with a specific responsive action by the other. In reciprocity formulations, explicit tradeoffs are emphasized (e.g., if you pick up your clothes, I'll make sure the bed linen is changed regularly).

41

In an equity conceptualization, what is important is the "bottom line," i.e., *over time,* work, domestic and emotional tasks must feel fairly distributed in the relationship. Rapoport and Rapoport (1975) indicate that a feeling of "fairness in the allocation of constraints" as well as in perceived benefits from the relationship is important. In the case example, Susan's current sense of having been "ripped off" by John suggests that her perception of a state of inequity is partly responsible for their current marital difficulties. Therapeutic efforts to help the marriage could usefully focus on restoring a sense of fairness in the relationship. Expectations of future as well as present spouse behavior usually need to conform to the principle of equity for a sustained sense of marital well-being.

Bailyn (1973) suggests that the spouses' concept of equity will vary at different points throughout the marital life cycle. Therefore, renegotiation will likely be necessary at times. A case study is presented below to illustrate the adaptive aspects of one dual-career couple's relationship, and how equity considerations were instrumental in helping them to change patterns of behavior. The case also amplifies how many of the personality characteristics of dual-career spouses, as discussed in this chapter, can lead to an understanding and facilitation of each spouse's growth and development.

Case #5. Julie and Ted have been married for seven years and have a daughter Amy, age 6. Julie is 29 years old and Ted is 31. They entered marital therapy with the expressed wish for help in improving their sexual relationship. At this point, their respective emotional roles in the marriage seemed rather fixed and stereotyped. Ted was perceived by both as being the solid, somewhat stoic and reliable partner. Julie was seen by both as the expressive, spontaneous, and creative spouse. They acknowledged that they were attracted to one another partly because each perceived the other as having something important to offer, partly along the lines of the above perceived personality characteristics.

To the therapist, it was evident early in therapy that the stereotyped notions each spouse held of the other didn't fit with much of each individual's behavior. Julie held a responsible job in the social service area, and was able to remain calm and unflappable in situations of crisis that were dysfunctional for her co-workers. Ted was emotional and creatively improvising in his interactions with Amy, who, in many ways, preferred father to mother as a playmate. One effect of placing one another in stereotyped "boxes" was a mutual felt dissatisfaction with their sex life. Julie had more premarital sexual experience than Ted. She criticized his wish to stay with the tried and true, rather than being willing to experiment in trying new and/or different modes of sexual expression in foreplay or intercourse. Julie admitted that Ted was a sensitive and patient lover, however, and she was usually orgastic and felt physically, if not emotionally, fulfilled after they made love. He felt her pressure to do different things sexually, but was not quite sure or comfortable with what he perceived her to want in this regard. He was puzzled over her unhappiness, which had gradually decreased his own sense of sexual satisfaction in the relationship. He readily agreed with Julie's suggestion that they seek sexual counseling.

The couple was seen for twelve therapy sessions, with two follow-up meetings, three months and nine months later. Their sexual relationship improved, as they were able to free themselves from the notion that Julie was "expressive" and Ted was "stoic." They were encouraged initially to alternate control of the sexual relationship (Kaplan, 1974). One week, Ted was in charge of initiating sex and Julie agreed to go along with his wishes, as long as she did not feel abused or exploited. The next week, Julie was in charge and Ted agreed to comply with her wishes, given the same proviso. They were encouraged during such periods to act out sexual fantasies they found exciting but had felt reluctant previously to carry out with one another (Sager, 1976). These behavioral procedures worked effectively to free both partners from the notion that Julie was inherently more sexual than Ted and that, based on this, they were sexually mismatched. In addition, Ted was able to share in therapy some troubling feelings he had been suppressing for some time about Julie's more extensive premarital sexual experience. This aspect of her background did not bother him from a moral standpoint, but caused him to fear not being able to meet her standards. Julie's dissatisfaction with their sexual relationship seemed to be a confirmation for Ted of this expectation. By talking this out, Julie was able to reassure Ted that she did find him appealing sexually, particularly in line with the new ways of sexual interaction he was initiating during the weeks in which he was in charge of their sexual relationship. He gradually began to see that Julie's prior relationship experiences led to her fuller development as a person and, indeed, he found himself wishing that he had had more serious relationships with other women prior to their marriage. The follow-up sessions indicated a sustained sense of improvement in the sexual area, as well as a notion of what they needed to do if things began to get routine.

The marriage of this couple was unusual, not in terms of their presenting sexual problem, but in the flexibility, basic commitment and level of understanding shown to one another. Ted had come from a farm background and was the oldest of four children. Everybody in the family had assigned chores from an early age, and there was a strong emphasis placed on family cooperation and harmony. The family was active in their church, which also offered most of their social contacts and outlets. Ted was especially good at math and his father carefully explained the financial aspects of the farm to him, perhaps expecting that his oldest son would eventually take over the management of the operation. Ted preferred city life, however, and remained in the town where he went to college, taking a job as a business manager with a small but thriving company.

Julie's family experience had been a generally happy one. She felt her father had been a bit too passive, and subject to her mother's domination, but she indicated that "in times of confrontation, he could hold his own." Julie had an older sister and a younger brother. She remained in close contact with her family (who lived in a small town approximately fifteen miles away) and continued to use her mother as an occasional confidante and babysitter for Amy. Ted liked Julie's parents and did not seem troubled by Julie's continuing emotional closeness to her mother.

The couple agreed before getting married that it would be all right if they had children early. In this manner, Amy "was and was not planned." After Amy was born, Julie took six weeks' maternity leave from her job. She felt very restless during this period, and sensed an urgency to get back to her job. These feelings resulted in the couple delaying having a second child, to the point where they were now uncertain as to whether they wanted any more children.

Toward the end of the twelve therapy sessions, Ted began to bring up the idea of his quitting his job to return to school. He expressed the wish to study technical aspects of agriculture, so

44

that he might eventually be able to help farmers with their production. He realized that his father had appreciated the technical advice garnered from such individuals during the years when Ted was growing up. Julie was receptive to Ted's wish to return to school, even though it would mean a period of financial sacrifice for the family. She stated: "Well, if that's what he wants to do, it's okay with me. We'll work it out. I don't think he ever really left the farm anyway, if you know what I mean. So it doesn't surprise me he wants to go back."

The therapist was frankly surprised at Julie's receptivity to this potential major alteration in their income and life-style. Her support of Ted's wishes seemed remarkably free of ambivalent feelings. When the observation was made that she seemed freely supportive of Ted's wishes, she replied: "I know he'd do the same thing for me if I wanted to go back to school. We've even talked about that possibility, but I'm happy where I am. And, also, he's helped me out a lot with Amy; here's a chance where I can help him out and I don't resent it, at least I don't think I do."

Nine months later, at the time of the second follow-up phone conversation, Julie reported that Ted was "back in graduate school and enjoying it." She continued: "Our lives have changed somewhat, we're sharing Amy's care more. Ted is home in the late afternoon to be with her. Then I take over in the evening, after supper, so he can study. All in all, it's working out."

As indicated earlier, at the time of the nine-month follow-up, both partners reported general satisfaction with their sexual relationship. There was an occasional tendency to fall back on the old pattern (Ted being contented with greater regularity in their sexual relating, Julie wishing for more variety). Both spouses, however, could express their feelings openly in this regard, and then contract to change things by talking about how to introduce more variety into their lovemaking. This was felt to be a mutual responsibility (and of potential mutual benefit) rather than a reflection that only one partner needed to change his or her behavior in order to improve things.

The relationship between Ted and Julie illustrates several personality features and motivating forces seen commonly in the behavior of dual-career spouses. In contrast to many dual-career couples seen in therapy, Julie and Ted showed greater flexibility of behavior and sensitivity to each other's needs, and a strong commitment to making their relationship work. Although they were seen for a relatively brief time in therapy (twelve sessions), it was possible to make some correlations with their background experiences and present marital behaviors.

Both partners grew up in families where they perceived their parents' marriage to be a happy one, though different in character from their own relationship. For example, neither Ted's nor Julie's mother was employed outside the home. Due to the nature of the farm operation, however, Ted's mother was perceived to be an equally contributing partner with her husband in providing economically and materially for the family. Julie sensed her mother "would have been happier if she had worked." She added: "Women didn't have quite the opportunity and support for getting a job back then that they do today. I thought sometimes she nagged at my father because she felt frustrated from being at home all day with the kids. We've talked about this, but now she says she's too old to go to work."

Julie seemed aware that the urgency associated with her own career involvement (seen in her restlessness during the six weeks of maternity leave after Amy was born) could be a partial carry-over from her mother's implied personal dissatisfactions. This awareness also helped her appreciate Ted's need for fulfillment in his career and may have enabled her to support with relatively little ambivalence his desire for a career change. In this manner, both spouses appeared to have an appreciation of the need for achievement and for the enhancement of self-esteem needs through occupational endeavors. A sense of perceived fairness or equity, in terms of the marriage having benefited both partners' development, was evident in the flexibility shown by one partner in adapting to the other's desired changes.

Ted and Julie had a firm commitment to their relationship at the time they began therapy. There may well have been some uncertainty about their choice of one another early in the marriage. The decision to have a child early may have served the purpose of solidifying their commitment to one another. It was clear that Amy was a source of gratification and emotional bonding for both Julie and Ted, and this was confirmed in their willingness to share the responsibility for their daughter's care. The therapist observed a warm and generally comfortable interaction between Amy and her parents during an early therapy session, arranged after the therapist had expressed a request to see the whole family at least for one visit. This session had also been important in gathering data to support the therapist's hypothesis that the stereotyped conceptions of Julie as "expressive" and Ted as "stoic" did not square with certain aspects of their behavior. It will be recalled that such labeling seemed in part responsible for the complaint of increasing sexual dissatisfaction that had led Ted and Julie to enter therapy.

In summary, focusing on underlying personality dynamics is helpful for understanding individuals likely to choose a dual-career life-style. A strong need for achievement, reliance on an extrinsic reward system (promotions, spouse recognition of efforts), hesitancy in making sustained interpersonal commitments and vulnerability to self-esteem injury through dependency frustration and fear of failure are common psychological characteristics. Partly as a result of these personality factors, there is usually a concern with whether aspects of the relationship (career opportunities, shared domestic responsibilities) are working out fairly for *both* spouses. Partners get into difficulty when these or other important aspects of the relationship are perceived as being inequitable in character. Given the relative newness of this life-style, and the usual accompanying lack of role models, it may be difficult for a dual-career couple who experience marital stress to work out their relationship problems satisfactorily on their own. Subsequent chapters will elaborate specific conflict areas and focus on psychotherapeutic intervention in dual-career marriage, including consideration of a variety of treatment strategies likely to benefit such couples.

·5·

Structural Problems in the Dual-Career Marriage

THE LACK of experiential role models for most dual-career couples has been noted. A further implication of this is the absence of established normative guidelines which can be used by such couples for dealing with common marital circumstances, such as having and caring for children, and dealing with the social demands and expectations of both careers.

Adapting to the demands of the dual-career life-style requires much flexibility from both partners, as well as a willingness to experiment and innovate. For example, if the couple have children, there are times when it will be necessary for one parent to stay home and take care of an ailing child. Such decisions usually need to be made with less than optimal advance notice. Solving this and other periodic dilemmas requires both partners to be flexible and not bound by conventional expectations (e.g., in the above case, convention would dictate that the wife stay home).

Husar and Grant (1968) found that dual-career couples, in general, were higher in reported self-actualization and perceived flexibility. (It is important to note, however, that the couples in this study were relatively older and more professionally established.) In terms of perceived equity, the "sacrifices" that each spouse makes in situations, such as the example with the sick child presented above, need to balance out over time, or resentment and felt exploitation by one partner is likely to ensue and lead to relationship problems.

In many ways, *a successful dual-career marriage needs to create its own structure over time. The structural guidelines which apply to traditional marriage are often not very helpful.* There is much room for conflict to occur as this process of structural evolution usually proceeds somewhat haphazardly. This chapter will explore potential structural dilemmas for dual-career couples by focusing on three major representative areas: (a) dealing with children; (b) management of time (alone and together); and (c) handling relationships with other people. In most marriages, the partners must deal with each of these issues; however, when both spouses have careers, certain unique problems are introduced into the situation. These will be elaborated below.

DEALING WITH CHILDREN

Having children introduces into a dual-career marriage certain pressures toward normalization. This happens, in part, because the presence of a child can easily pull the partners back toward more traditional sex-role behaviors and expectations. The assumption of parental roles usually magnifies certain gender-linked expectations. Traditionally, mothers are expected to take care of babies and children, and, even if the father provides a great deal of help with this, the major responsibility usually falls to the mother (Johnson and Johnson, 1977). Over time, this can easily upset the carefully achieved equitable balance of domestic tasks and responsibilities which may have been achieved by the partners in a dual-career marriage, leading to conflict and the felt need for a restructuring of the relationship (Rapoport and Rapoport, 1975).

Many couples who have worked out a functional system that enables each partner to balance relationship and career demands have difficulty once they become parents. Even couples who try a parental role reversal based on spouse preference (husband takes care of home and children while wife works full time) or who attempt shared parenting (each partner works half time and is home half time) find that social pressures and expectations can insidiously undermine their thoughtfully constructed system. Both spouses get tired of explaining why they are "doing it this way" and may feel increased doubts in the face of constant questions from relatives, friends, and employers. Feelings of guilt and the expectation that "it's not going to work" easily creep into the relationship. In the area of child rearing, perhaps more than any other, societal norms and expectations seem to work against dual-career marriages. Given this, it is not surprising that dual-career couples tend to have fewer children on the average than couples in traditional marriages (Holmstrom, 1972). Moreover, Rapoport and Rapoport (1971) and St. John-Parsons (1978) found an emphasis in all dual-career families studied on enhancing the independence and competence of the children. Parents reported satisfaction over their children's mastery and aspiration to a high level of accomplishment.

It is important that the parents not set the expectation of independent behavior beyond the developmental capabilities of the child. Children must, after all, be permitted to be children. Since a high degree of mature behavior demonstrating the child's capacity to function independently often meshes with dual-career parental needs, a strong demand characteristic is created. The child may then feel as if age-appropriate dependent behaviors must be suppressed. An adaptive pattern of pseudomaturity can follow. Later in the child's development (perhaps in adolescence) regressive, dependent and attention-seeking acting-out behaviors may appear. It is not always possible at that later point to relate such acting-out behaviors directly to the frustration of earlier age-appropriate dependency strivings.

It is important for dual-career parents to be sensitive to what their children can and cannot handle in terms of independence demonstrating behaviors. Taking time regularly to tune in on the child's feelings about what is being expected of him or her is essential. The time demands of each spouse's career often mean that the child will be left with a variety of other caretakers. This underscores the need for regular periods of communication between parent and child about mutual expectations. These talk sessions are both necessary and helpful for providing continuity in the child's life.

There are very few empirical studies of children in dual-career families. Johnson and Johnson (1977) interviewed separately 28 spouses in such families who had at least one child under the age of 12 (mean number of children was 1.7). The average age of the children in these families was 5.6 years. In all 28 families, the "wives retained the major responsibility in most areas of child rearing" (Johnson and Johnson, 1977, p. 393). This meant that having children required the wife to make relatively more career adjustments and sacrifices than the husband. As might be expected, this resulted in a certain amount of conflict and role strain for the wives in the study. The strain was caused by the often incompatible demands of home and work, e.g., the previously mentioned issue of which spouse stays home with a sick child.

Consistent with other studies of dual-career families (Holmstrom, 1972; Rapoport and Rapoport, 1971), the couples interviewed by Johnson and Johnson denied *overt* marital conflict arising from this somewhat inequitable situation. Indeed, only 2 of the 28 families (7.14%) "gave responses that indicated sufficient marital conflict to interfere with the (perceived) mutually supportive relationship" (Johnson and Johnson, 1977, p. 393). In other words, the conflicts generated by the demands of child rearing were not perceived by the spouses to spill over into the marriage. At the same time, the "role strain for the wives involved fatigue, emotional depletion, and in some cases, guilt" (p. 393). It is difficult to see how these feelings would not over time lead to some marital conflict. At the very least, they sound like a prescription for felt martyrdom on the part of the wives. (The husbands in the study were able to resolve any perceived role strain by denying it or using rationalizations to minimize its effects, e.g., seeing trouble with the children as "just a phase" the child was going through.) Based on the degree of reported high marital adjustment and perceived spouse support, Johnson and Johnson conclude that "the source of strain can be identified with child rearing, not the marriage relationship" (p. 393).

The author's experience with dual-career couples in marital therapy, in partial contrast to the above findings, suggests that the *marriage* is indeed likely to suffer as a by-product of the wife's experiencing role strain. The Johnson and Johnson study is consistent, however, with much of the literature on dual-career marriage in which the spouses deny marital conflict. Such findings stand in contrast to the picture seen in clinical practice, where felt conflict leads a number of dual-career couples to seek professional help.

As applied to child rearing, an understanding of the need to deny marital conflict may be explained in terms of a reduction of cognitive dissonance (Festinger, 1957). In other words, dual-career couples who have children may need to convince themselves that their marriage and their children are "doing fine." For the wives, this could be one way of gaining reassurance that despite their doing a traditionally anormal thing (having both a career and a family), they had achieved success at both endeavors.

51

Such a belief system would be consistent with the high needs for achievement found in such individuals (see Chapter 4). The fantasy of familial bliss can be rudely shattered if the child begins to show some effects of the family's role strain. The disruption of this defensive process can be seen in Case #6, which follows.

Object relations theory (Stewart, Peters, Marsh and Stewart, 1975) provides a particularly useful framework for understanding some of the defense mechanisms used by the parents in dealing with problems encountered by their children. Three of these mechanisms, (a) projective identification, (b) splitting, and (c) collusion, are defined in the following case study and examples are presented.

Case #6. Ron and Claire, a couple in their early forties, have two children, a daughter Becky, age 12, and a son, Jimmy, age 14. They are both occupationally successful individuals, at least by others' standards, and pride themselves on being good parents despite a mutually acknowledged unsatisfying marriage (which led to their seeking counseling). The partners had met during the period of their professional training and married after a courtship of a year and a half. There was a great deal of "image fixation" early in their relationship; both saw themselves as socially responsible individuals who, by bonding together, would jointly, and, perhaps, synergistically, tackle some of the social evils and injustices in the world.

When both took jobs, had children, and settled into the routine of home and work, their original attractive images were strained. Instead of the exciting, involved and active person each thought he or she had married, each spouse began to perceive the other as dull, burned out and, at times, quite lazy. Resentment over feeling let down led to mutual alienation in the affectional part of the relationship. This was accompanied by a good deal of projective identification in which each would project the fear of what he or she had become (as contrasted with the prior "image") onto the other and then attack the spouse for having those undesirable qualities. Felt impotence in their respective careers was an example of this; each would constantly and subtly remind the other how he or she had lost the respect of colleagues.

Both parents, however, remained devoted to their children despite, or as a substitute for, their marital dissatisfactions. A good deal of time and energy was devoted by mother to daughter and father to son, with relatively little management and limit-setting of the other child by the opposite parent. There were times when mother accused father of spoiling his son and a comparable number of occasions where father cast similar criticism at mother for the way she treated her daughter. On the whole, though, the parents felt they were doing a good job of raising their children and even took pride in the belief that their marital antagonisms had not "affected the children."

Their use of denial was severely tested when Jimmy began to engage in a variety of inappropriate behaviors beyond the limits of usual adolescent acting out, i.e., bullying younger kids, associating with peers who were into drugs and petty thievery, and not working up to his previously demonstrated performance in school. Their puzzlement was compounded by the fact that Becky had remained a "model child," e.g., doing well in school and having lots of friends. Claire's initial tendency was to blame Ron's child-rearing indulgences for Jimmy's change in behavior, ignoring the fact that she had been comparably lenient with Becky and that this had not led to similar problems for her daughter. Ron had little defense against Claire's criticism and began to introject the blame, adding felt failure as a parent on top of similar doubts regarding his stagnant career.

The "splitting" (Stewart et al., 1975) of the parents into caretaker roles for their different children permitted the wife in this instance to avoid taking responsibility for her son's changed behavior. The defensive separating of the marital and family realms also diverted the spouses from any notion that Jimmy's difficulties could be a partial reflection of tensions in the marital relationship. The therapist was inclined to pursue the latter hypothesis, inferring that much of Jimmy's acting out could serve as (a) an indirect expression of Ron's hostility toward Claire, and (b) a counteraction to Claire's fear of the implications for herself of Ron's increasing psychological impotence and perceived inability to act effectively in changing the declining fortunes of his life and career. That is, having an active, assertive son (albeit somewhat inappropriately expressed) partly made up for perceived, projectively identified shortcomings in her husband.

Claire was also unaware of how she had colluded with Becky to let her daughter's "good" qualities compensate for Jimmy's "bad" ones. When Jimmy began to show difficulty, she would "turn him over" to Ron for discipline, which she unconsciously believed her husband was not capable of providing. However, she paid close attention to any hint of trouble on Becky's part, e.g., carefully helping her with homework whenever she would bring home schoolwork that showed even a few wrong answers. Part of Claire's behavior seemed to represent the common wish for perfection in one's children, as a partial compensation for perceived parental imperfections. Thus, "splitting" by the parents of the two children mirrored in many ways the marital distantiation experienced by the couple.

After approximately two months of couple therapy, the parents' concern over Jimmy's behavior began to mount, and the therapist started seeing the whole family. After six family sessions, during which both children expressed a desire for more realistic feedback and limit-setting by their parents (e.g., "You never said it was wrong to take drugs"), Jimmy's behavior began to show improvement. This seemed due, in part, to the parents developing an agreed-upon system of discipline and their setting consistent rules, as well as some breaking down of the collusion between father–son and mother–daughter. The therapist then resumed working with the couple. They could no longer focus their attention on Jimmy's (and Becky's) problems to avoid facing directly their marital dissatisfactions. Having to give up this defensive maneuver led to much therapeutic resistance and a retreat into their respective careers.

Although, in the final analysis, there was little gained from therapy in terms of increased intimacy in the relationship, some of the felt hostility diminished as both spouses adopted a sort of "live-and-let-live" attitude toward one another. Consequently, they felt less motivation to continue in therapy and terminated shortly thereafter. A six-month phone follow-up indicated that marital satisfaction was still low but that "the children are doing well."

During therapy, the therapist focused at times on what the couple's life would be like when their children were grown. Both could see that in some ways they were staying together "for the sake of the children." The wife, who expressed more *overt* concern regarding the emotional alienation in the marriage than did her husband, said that she might get a divorce after the children left home. However, the therapist sensed that both spouses were bound together in part by deep fears that each could not be loved and accepted by anyone else. In this sense, their emotional distance kept each spouse safe from risking exposure and thus testing out this felt underlying vulnerability. It could also explain why they remained married, despite their professed dissatisfaction. Their situation was not unlike that of the familiar George and Martha in Edward Albee's play, *Who's Afraid of Virginia Woolf?* In this light, it is not surprising that couples such as Ron and Claire may remain married, even after their children have left home.

In contrast with many dual-career couples, Ron and Claire were unable to support one another for the mutual benefit of thier respective careers. Each needed the other's achievement partly as a defense against his or her own fear of failure. The up-and-down character of both their career fortunes was perceived as personally threatening and reacted to by attack and condemnation instead of by support and understanding. Given this coldness between the partners, it is perhaps not surprising that Jimmy and Becky became their respective "best friend." Both Claire and Ron had subtly punitive parents (his mother and her father) who put high achievement expectations on them in a partial attempt to make up for the parents' own felt failure in life. The turning to their children for much of their emotional gratification might be understood as a response to the feeling that they had disappointed adult figures (parents, professional colleagues, professors in school, etc.) by their felt lack of accomplishment. They expected that their children would be less judgmental, at least while they were young and dependent. Hopefully, therapy helped to diminish the potential for prolonged emotional exploitation of their children, even if it did not directly improve felt satisfaction within the marriage.

MANAGING TIME

A frequent complaint of individuals in dual-career marriages is the lack of time, both to be alone and to be together (Holmstrom, 1972). This problem is compounded if the couple has children and it is magnified by the individuals' high needs for achievement. Thus, they spend more hours working (at the office and at home) than is necessary for reasonable occupational success, at least as defined by others' standards. This situation can be exacerbated when the couple becomes destructively competitive (see Chapter 6), each trying to outachieve the other, putting more and more time and energy into their work while withdrawing emotionally from the relationship.

To the outside observer, the daily life of a dual-career family is likely to seem frenetic at worst and superorganized at best. Successful functioning within this life-style is likely to require careful planning and organization by all family members. Most families take advantage of the higher level of income resulting from two careers to hire additional domestic and child-care help (Holmstrom, 1972). However, society does not always cooperate with the vicissitudes of this aberrant life-style, e.g., the scheduling of no school on working days or when inclement weather results in young children being let out of school early.

Any difficulty or reluctance on the part of dual-career couples to carefully plan and organize their lives is likely to lead to marital conflict (St. John-Parsons, 1978). Yet a fair number of couples, particularly young ones, feel an aversion to having their life so completely structured. They attempt to cope with the many and oftentimes conflicting demands of work and home with little more than a random schedule of who does what and when. There seems to be a trust in "good will" to promote cooperation and get everything done. However, not being able to organize and schedule effectively seems destined eventually to destroy whatever "good faith" may have been carefully built up between the partners. The lack of a detailed schedule is also a likely prescription for felt inequity; sooner or later one spouse will feel he or she is doing more than the other and will tend to resent it.

Filling one's life with the demands of work and home can also be a way of dealing with conflicts in the area of intimacy. It is easy for both partners in a dual-career marriage to throw themselves into their work. Given our work-oriented society, it seems easy and natural to justify putting much effort and energy into one's occupation. To the clinician, the defensive aspects of this behavior are evident. For example, a couple may find time for everything but being together. A common result of this pattern is that the sexual aspect of their relationship becomes less frequent and somewhat perfunctory. The turning to one's children for gratification of needs for adult closeness can also be a common response to intimacy conflicts, as elaborated in the case of Ron and Claire, presented earlier.

The marital therapist is often called upon to help couples who feel they have drifted apart. With dual-career couples, one helpful first step in this process is a careful assessment of how they are using their time. A case study will illustrate some of the difficulties a couple can face in this area, as well as some steps that can be taken to help ameliorate the situation.

Case #7. Frank and Ellen are in their late twenties and have three small children, daughters ages 7 and 5, and a son, age 4. They had married early, when Ellen found out she was pregnant. The other two children "just happened, we didn't plan them." They had settled into a traditional marriage, with Ellen taking care of home and children and Frank pursuing his career in the social service field. While Frank was doing well and enjoying satisfying work relationships with both male and female colleagues, Ellen was becoming increasingly desperate and depressed. She was feeling "tied down" at an early age and exhausted by the demands of three small children. She had begun recently to work on a half-time basis as a hospital aide, but did not find the work satisfying or challenging. She acknowledged that she "took the job just to get out of the house for a while." Frank helped around the house, but did little to truly relieve Ellen of her home and family responsibilities.

Ellen's abortive suicide gesture brought the couple into therapy. Following a fight over his being late from an athletic function, Ellen locked herself in the bedroom and told Frank she was about to take a handful of Sominex. He pleaded with her to let him in and to talk things over, which she did. The next day Frank called their family doctor to get the name of a therapist for Ellen. The physician, sensing marital problems, gave them the name of a marital therapist and suggested it would be a good idea for them to go together.

Ellen talked openly of her felt desperation and announced that she had made plans to go back to college "whether Frank likes it or not," now that their youngest child was in nursery school during part of the day. She had abandoned her prior career plans and had quit college in her sophomore year when she decided to get married. Frank offered little resistance to her newly formulated educational plan, even in the face of the therapist's suggestion that Ellen's resumption of her education would call for some careful restructuring of the couple's time, task and resource distribution. She felt better, having made the decision to return to school, and was pleased with his acceptance, albeit somewhat passive, of her idea. They decided to try things on their own and left therapy after three sessions.

Approximately eight months later, Ellen (now in school on a full-time basis) called to say that she and Frank were still having problems and would like to come back to therapy. During the initial session, Ellen complained that their communication had begun to suffer; she was puzzled by this, since she felt happier with her life. One of the therapist's first questions had to do with how the couple had reallocated their time and domestic activities to cope with Ellen's going back to school. She said that Frank was helping out more with the cooking and that he "has been real good about taking care of the children." The children had apparently adjusted well to the change in the household routine and it soon became apparent to the therapist that the main casualty of their new situation was the couple's time together. The felt breakdown in communication seemed partly a by-product of this.

In terms of the time demands, Frank and Ellen were operating without a formal schedule. Ellen stated: "We just see what needs doing and do it." This had worked for a while but was becoming increasingly unsatisfactory. Both spouses cited instances where a task was not being done (e.g., Tommy, age 4, had too many pants with holes in them—Ellen's job—or the storm windows were not being taken down and it was already June—Frank's responsibility). The therapist suggested that they attempt to draw up a more formal time and task schedule before the next session. This suggestion was met with nods of agreement by both spouses and the conversation went on to other topics. However, when several similar complaints surfaced a few sessions later, the therapist again inquired about "the schedule." Despite good intentions, they had not gotten around to "writing things down." Choosing to override the passive resistance implied by their behavior, at this point, the therapist indicated a willingness to help them make out a schedule. The couple agreed and a schedule was constructed, with care taken to assure that domestic and child-care tasks were felt to be equitably distributed (after much give-and-take discussion by the partners).

The therapist, cognizant of the couple's inability to find time for one another, suggested building a place for this into the schedule. Ellen agreed but Frank was hesitant, replying, "Does that mean we *have* to talk to one another?" The therapist chose to ignore for the moment the symptomatic implications of Frank's question (in particular, the ambivalence he might be feeling toward Ellen's returning to school and the fear that he might find out, from talking with her, that he was married now to a "different person," and maybe one who didn't need him as much). The therapist replied to Frank's question: "That is simply half an hour each day for you to be together. You can use it however you wish. You may want to take turns, with Frank deciding what you will do on one day and Ellen, the next. If you want to talk then, fine. But you may wish to do something else, such as listen to music, take a walk, or even something a little 'crazy', like fooling around or having a playful pillow fight. But it's important for many busy couples to know they will have this time together and can count on it being scheduled into their daily activities."

Frank and Ellen followed the therapist's suggestion and decided on nine to nine-thirty P.M., after the kids were in bed and before they "konked out" for the evening. They reported that the first few evenings felt a little awkward, as they had literally gotten away from being together. But things gradually became more comfortable and a more natural spontaneity in planning times and activities together replaced the fixed schedule after a few weeks.

In summary, dual-career couples often report difficulty in finding meaningful time together. The marital therapist should be alert to many defensive aspects of this condition, particularly in terms of taking extra time for work or overinvolvement with one's children as a way of avoiding marital relationship conflicts in the area of intimacy. Many dual-career couples are able to sustain a meaningful level of emotional interaction through careful scheduling and organization and by employing outside help for certain domestic and child-care tasks. Time for the relationship is essential, as well as time for oneself. The therapist can help the partners in the achievement of this balance, often through such practical devices as assisting them in making out an equitable time schedule. Another example of this process, with excerpts from one of the therapy sessions, is presented in Chapter 8.

RELATIONSHIPS WITH OTHERS

There are several reasons why dual-career couples tend to lead restricted social lives. Prominent among these would be the great and often conflicting time demands placed on both partners. In addition, there may be some wish to limit social contacts with couples who do not represent similar life-styles. Rapoport and Rapoport (1971) indicate that the friends of the dual-career families in their study were most often other dual-career couples. They mention the wish to avoid subtle censure and guilt induction, especially in the wife, from individuals with different values (e.g., the criticism implied in the question, "How do you find time to work with small children?"). Hopefully, such social criticism will diminish in the face of the rapidly increasing incidence of dual-career marriage.

The greatest amount of social interaction with others usually comes from dual-career partners' relationships with colleagues at work. Their jobs serve as an introit to a social network of people who share common interests. Having a ready source of social interaction during the day can lead to lessened desire on the part of both individuals for extrawork friends and social outlets. At times, this results in less interaction with one another. The situation is a somewhat mixed blessing and Ingmar Bergman's movie, *Scenes from a Marriage,* provides a vivid illustration of the advantages and disadvantages brought about by this.

The main characters in the movie, Johan (an experimental psychologist) and Marianne (an attorney specializing in divorce cases), find their belief of marital bliss severely tested when the marriage of their friends falls apart. Johan and Marianne then realize that involvements with their families and with colleagues have left them with little meaningful time together. Johan, in particular, interprets this state of affairs as meaning that much of their relationship has been a sham and decides to leave Marianne for another woman. The process of separation and eventual divorce is prolonged and painful for both Johan and Marianne.

Several years later, while married to other individuals, they begin an affair with one another. In this new relationship, they are together out of felt choice and the movie ends with their experiencing a reassurance of their mutual caring and a revitalization of their emotional bonding. (An expanded psychological analysis of this movie and its implications for contemporary marriage can be found in the article by Plone, 1975).

On the one hand, having ready access to a social network may help to avoid the struggle many couples go through in regard to which partner is going to be the "social chairperson" for the marriage. Both husband and wife have a set of colleagues with whom they can easily arrange social engagements. On the other hand, the availability of colleagues as a ready source of friends can cause a number of problems for the couple. For example, it may reinforce the tendency alluded to earlier for individuals in dual-career marriages to withdraw from the relationship and overinvest in their work. That is, social as well as occupational needs can be met at work and this, a traditional source of friction in marriages where one partner works, can be compounded when both spouses are employed.

In clinical practice, the greatest problem encountered in the social relationship area relates to the natural forming of close relationships with one's colleagues and resultant spouse jealousy. This can become a critical test of the strength of the marriage and the personal security of the individuals involved. It was noted in Chapter 3 that dual-career couples may have purposely restricted their earlier social relationships in order to pursue advanced education which could lead to a career. Their choice of a marital partner was often based on propinquity and similarity of values in the career area rather than on the ultimate choosing of one person after many relationship experiences. As a consequence, many individuals in dual-career marriages find the acceptance, respect and affection accorded by their colleagues to be quite attractive. There may be a wish to form close relationships partly as a way of "making up for lost time" in the social area. The potential for this is enhanced by the presence of co-workers who share similar professional interests and values, and are thus in a position to provide much ego gratification and reinforcement.

Couples often come into therapy when their relationship boundaries are threatened by the formation of close relationships with other people. These are especially upsetting if sexual experience has been revealed or even if fantasies along these lines have been shared with one's spouse. The ready availability of potential sexual partners for *both* spouses can magnify the fear and further strain the marriage. The therapist needs to help such couples work through the fears and arrive at an agreement, if possible, about the boundaries of their relationship. Failure to do this is destined generally to drive the partners away from one another and enhance the fantasied attractiveness of other relationships. The following case study illustrates some of the difficulties dual-career couples can encounter in the area of social relationships.

Case #8. Alice and Jeff had married in their middle twenties while both were in graduate school. Both had strong wishes to have children and it was decided mutually that Alice would work part time after finishing her graduate studies, so that they could start a family.

When the couple entered marital therapy, they were in their late thirties, had been married for fifteen years and had two children, a son, age 13, and a daughter, age 10. Jeff had established himself comfortably in his occupation and was respected by his peers. Alice had resumed work on a nearly full-time basis during the past five years. She was popular with her co-workers, who often came to her for advice about personal problems. She was seen by others as a mature individual who was managing successfully to have both a career and a family.

Shortly after the birth of their second child, Jeff found himself increasingly attracted to Carla, a woman colleague, who reported dissatisfaction with her own marriage. After many long talks, they revealed their mutual intense feelings for one another but decided against having an affair "in order to just remain friends." Jeff felt guilty about his feelings toward Carla, and after much soul-searching told Alice about them. Alice was surprisingly accepting of what had happened, although she was reassured by the fact that Jeff and Carla had not had a sexual relationship. Alice had sustained a tolerance of Carla's "presence" in Jeff's life during the past approximately nine years.

The stimulus for Jeff and Alice to enter therapy was an increase in felt emotional distance during the past five years. This troubled Alice more than Jeff, and he had been less responsive than she would have liked to her efforts to talk about what had happened to their relationship. Jeff did agree to enter marital therapy, but from the start conveyed the impression that he thought their troubles were "her problem." He still maintained his friendship with Carla and did not see this as competing with his feelings toward Alice. Because both partners could not agree on "the problem," their motivation for marital therapy decreased, and they stopped coming. Alice, however, asked to meet with the therapist for several individual sessions, in what appeared to be a wish for reassurance that her feelings about the marriage were justified. Jeff was supportive of Alice's wish and a period of short-term individual therapy began.

In the individual sessions, Alice expressed the strong belief that "Jeff isn't going to change." She then talked about her feelings of attraction for a colleague (Bill), with whom she was engaged in several joint projects. She was acutely aware that Bill's openness to sharing feelings and "his sensitivity" were attractive to her in part because "these are the qualities I want from Jeff." She continued: "Jeff used to show them to me but I don't know what's happened. He talks like he lets Carla see that part of him." In accordance with her agreement with Jeff regarding outside sexual relationships, she had not begun an affair with Bill, although he indicated a willingness in this regard. She shared with Jeff her experiences in this new relationship, but soft-pedaled any notion that she might be doing it out of spite, i.e., to punish Jeff for not meeting her intimacy needs. He accepted her relationship with Bill and, indeed, felt some assuagement of the guilt he had over his deep affection for Carla. Alice terminated therapy shortly thereafter, feeling better about herself and her marriage, although she had not reported any substantial increase in emotional intimacy within the relationship. The therapist suggested they meet once more, a few months later, for a follow-up session.

At the time of follow-up, Alice reported that things were "pretty much the same" in regard to her marriage. She had, however, increased the amount of time she was spending with Bill and had arranged a great deal of overlap in their professional activities. She said that neither she nor Bill felt their respective marriages were threatened by this. Indeed, she presented the arrangement as a workable solution to the lack of emotional intimacy in her relationship with Jeff. As all parties seemed happy, the therapist decided not to pursue this further, beyond noting (silently) that he, himself, could probably not be happy in such a marital arrangement.

In summary, the presence of colleagues and a ready social network for both individuals is seen as a mixed blessing for dual-career couples. Problems can occur when there is a tendency to withdraw emotionally from the marriage as a consequence of the ego gratification offered in outside relationships. Therapists can help the couple to maintain a balance in this regard, preserving or enhancing marital intimacy while facilitating a climate in which each partner can enjoy the benefits of close relationships with others. Negotiation and/or revision of the couple's contract vis-à-vis outside relationships can often be helpful. Such a process is too often done on a *post hoc* basis (i.e., after one or the other of the partners has formed a relationship that poses some threat to the marital boundaries).

In this chapter, three prominent structural problem areas in dual-career marriage (issues with children, time management, and relationships with others) have been elaborated. These structural areas can relate to more generic patterns of conflict in dual-career marriage—e.g., underlying power struggles—and these are discussed in the following chapter.

·6·

Conflict Syndromes

MOST PRIOR STUDIES of dual-career marriage have shown a tendency for husband and wife to deny continuing, disruptive marital conflict (Paloma, 1972; Hopkins and White, 1978). Various reasons for this have been discussed in previous chapters, e.g., to reduce cognitive dissonance surrounding the conflicting demands of job and family, and to avoid having to deal directly with perceived inequities in the relationship. Focusing on areas of conflict is not meant to exclude the generally agreed-upon benefits of this life-style. For many individuals, marriage in which both partners have careers is a freely chosen and preferred form of marriage. There may be synergistic advantages, as seen in the Martin, Berry and Jacobsen (1975) study, where being married to another sociologist facilitated both partners' career development and achievements. Other commonly mentioned benefits of dual-career marriage include the possibility of enhanced intellectual companionship, greater material resources as a result of two incomes, and the possibility of both spouses feeling more self-fulfillment and contentment in their lives. An elaboration of the positive aspects of dual-career marriage is presented in Holmstrom (1972) and Rapoport and Rapoport (1971). The Rapoports also include a number of extended case studies of English couples, who provide a more intensive look at the daily vicissitudes of the dual-career life-style and its advantages and liabilities. The positive aspects of this marital style notwithstanding, as more dual-career couples seek marital therapy, information as to the source and nature of common problem areas should also prove helpful to counselors and therapists.

The present chapter will discuss three common major problem areas in dual-career marriage: (a) competition between spouses, (b) distribution of power in the marital relationship, and (c) arranging and maintaining a support structure. Although every married couple must, at times, deal with each of these issues, the problems they present for dual-career families are somewhat unique. These special aspects are the focus here.

ADJUSTMENT AND CONFLICT IN DUAL-CAREER MARRIAGE: A REVIEW

Two earlier studies concerned with the question of conflict in dual-career marriage are those of Garland (1972) and Paloma (1972). These authors report on different facets of a similar research project conducted in the late 1960s. The authors interviewed (separately and together) the spouses in 53 couples ranging in age from 20 to 60, where the wife held a high-level professional position (generally in academia, law or medicine).

On the whole, these researchers found that conflict was minimized in these marriages, due largely to the wife's accommodation. In almost all cases, she was willing to subordinate her career to that of her husband. Indeed, the few instances of reported conflict tended to involve those situations where the wife was achieving greater career success and/or was earning a higher income than her husband. The persuasiveness of the wife's accommodation was striking. "All except four of the female subjects made a conscious decision to place the home demands first on their list of priorities; these women were satisfied with the situation the way it was" (Paloma, 1972, p. 194).

From the husband's side, 20 of the 53 males (37.74%) were classified as having "traditional" expectations in that the wife's occupational commitments were seen by *both* spouses as clearly subordinate to her husband's and to family demands. Twenty-seven of the 53 males (50.94%) were classified as "neotraditional," where the wife's occupational situation was taken into account in the couples' major decisions (e.g., where the couple would settle geographically). However, role division in family and child-care matters tended to be along more or less traditional lines and generally followed gender-role stereotyped expectations. Five of the 53 couples (9.43%) were classified as "matriarchal," wherein the wife (sometimes unwillingly) exceeded the husband in terms of occupational accomplishments and income. Only one of the 53 couples (1.89%) was classified as "egalitarian," in the sense that "the significance of the spouse's biological sex is *reduced to an*

66

absolute minimum" (Garland, 1972, p. 202, italics added). By this the author meant that domestic and child-care tasks were shared equally by the couple and without regard to gender prescribed divisions or expectations. (As noted in Chapter 4, this is a common idea of what role sharing involves, but rarely is such a concept implemented in this manner. Equity rather than egalitarian considerations are seen as more commonly governing the behavior of couples who wish to share domestic and child-care duties.)

In summary, the dual-career spouses in the Garland and Paloma studies achieved a pattern of adaptation that minimized felt role strain and marital stress. This was generally achieved by the wife accommodating to domestic responsibilities and, in essence, holding two or three jobs (career, domestic, and child care) to her husband's one. Yet, the wives (and, not surprisingly, the husbands) generally reported satisfaction with this adaptive pattern and complained only of a lack of time and energy for being together as spouses, to the extent that each desired. Paloma concludes:

> It is quite significant that the data clearly suggest that the married professional woman is basically satisfied with life the way she lives it. Among the women interviewed, most found being a wife and mother very satisfying and taking precedence over their professional lives. Despite cries from radical feminists for the complete "emancipation" of women, most of our respondents showed no real desire for such emancipation. Their assertion is strong that in light of our contemporary social structure, the family must come first for a woman. Call them Aunt Tabbys if you will, but they seem quite satisfied with their lot (Paloma, 1972, p. 197).

It would seem important to repeat the Garland and Paloma studies to see if contemporary attitudes confirm their earlier findings. The present author's impression is that fewer married professional women are "satisfied with their (traditional) lot," and many more expect an equitable consideration from their spouses for their career situation. One needs also to consider the emancipation of men as well as women. Not a few husbands are finding that a reordering of priorities may mean putting family first and work second, particularly when they have young children. The study by Gronseth (1975), involving work and domestic sharing in Swedish couples, is presented in Chapter 10, exploring and elaborating this concept of male emancipation. In sum, changing social and personal expectations are causing marital conflict for a number of couples, who do not see the solution to the dilemma of who works and who stays home lying in the wife's accommodation and career subordination.

In addition to the question of whether the Paloma and Garland findings would still hold true, their work is subject to certain empirical criticism. They did not do a statistical analysis of their data, leaving the reader uncertain as to whether their results are statistically significant. In addition, as they note, the classification of their couples by subtype (traditional, neotraditional, etc.) and their judgments about the nature and extent of "role strain" were made jointly and subjectively by the authors themselves, leaving much room for experimenter bias and leading to potential difficulty in replication of their work. Their findings, which in many ways parallel those of Rapoport and Rapoport (1971), serve, however, as a historically useful anchor point for comparison of contemporary dual-career couples' attitudes and problems.

A well known sociologist, Talcott Parsons (1954), hypothesized that a marriage where the husband and wife were in the same profession was inherently unstable. This happened because Parsons believed it inevitably cast one spouse into destructive occupational role competition with the other. This was not found to be the case in the Garland and Paloma studies; however, as noted above, competition was often precluded by the wife's acceptance of a subordinate role occupationally, compared to that of her husband. Fortunately for the many co-professionals married to one another, Parsons' hypothesis has not been supported in empirical studies.

Martin, Berry and Jacobsen (1975) studied 86 husband–wife sociologists employed at the same academic institution. (It is not clear how many of these husbands and wives were employed in the same department, although presumably there were a number of instances where this was the case. The study sample involved the period 1969–1974, when nepotism rules were just beginning to be less rigidly enforced.) Martin et al. used as a control group other female sociologists, married and unmarried. In contrast to Parsons' prediction, they found that "compared to other females in the profession, sociologist wives were proportionally much more successful at obtaining their Ph.D., achieving higher academic ranks, gaining more promotions, avoiding demotions and practicing longer professional careers" (Martin et al., 1975, p. 742). Only in the temporal aspects of employment were sociologist wives at some disadvantage. That is, they were more likely to be employed on a half-time basis, compared to husbands and other female sociologists. The authors speculate that this may be a by-product of existent nepotism rules.

In explaining their findings and the disconfirmation of Parsons' hypothesis, Martin et al. point out that being married to a sociologist colleague was more likely to be professionally facilitative than destructive. This resulted primarily from the wife being able to take advantage of her husband's information and experience in order to facilitate working within the academic "system."

Martin et al. did not deal with personal conflicts engendered by being married to a co-professional. In their study, the husbands tended to be older, to have completed their Ph.D. sooner (by 4.4 years on the average), and to have secured an academic position prior to their wives' professional employment. Thus, husband and wife were rarely at the same rung on the academic ladder, and this perhaps helped mute direct competitive feelings. Such circumstances, however, might be expected to lead to jealousy, if not felt competitiveness, but Martin et al. did not report such a finding.

A comparable study (Bryson, Bryson, Licht and Licht, 1976; Bryson, Bryson and Johnson, 1978) deals with married psychologists. In this research, personality characteristics received a greater emphasis than in the Martin et al. study. On the whole, Bryson et al. confirmed the Martin et al. findings (and disconfirming Parsons' hypothesis), in that working within the same profession facilitated productivity for both husbands and wives.

In contrast to that reported but usually downplayed by couples in many of the prior studies of dual-career marriage, Bryson et al. found a variety of felt hindrances for the wife's career, that were self- or spouse-imposed. These included the familiar placing differential value on the husband's career and an inequitable division of domestic responsibilities. In regard to the latter, the authors state: "The only stereotypically female activity for which professional wives do not bear an absolute majority of responsibility is housecleaning, but only because outside help is employed rather than because husbands share the responsibility" (Bryson et al., 1976, p. 14). They concluded that the division of labor in professional pairs was relatively similar to that reported by control group wives, who were in essentially traditional marriages.

Overall, the psychologist wives tended to be more productive than other female psychologists (married or unmarried), but less productive than their husbands. They were also more likely to feel discriminated against (partly the result of nepotism rules) and were less satisfied with their careers than other women psychologists. These findings extend the results of Martin et al. and suggest that even though wives of co-professionals are more productive in terms of scholarly activity, they may well derive less personal felt satisfaction from their professional endeavors. However, this dissatisfaction is *not* perceived as a by-product of felt competition with their husbands. Both spouses see the source of dissatisfaction as related to realities outside the marriage. Bryson et al. postulate:

> A tentative model for organizing and explaining these data involves viewing the professional pair as a mutually facilitative and supportive unit whose goals are in conflict with external pressures. Each member of such a pair is motivated by the presence of the other and derives some satisfaction from the other's accomplishments as well as from his or her own. However, the shared and individual goals of each member of the pair conflict with the external realities of institutional regulations and domestic demands. These conflicts must be resolved in some way. Typically, this resolution is at least partially based on traditional sex roles, a division that is accepted by both members of the pair. Unfortunately, this division does not result in an equal sharing of the pressures, an effect that is most strikingly revealed in the wife's perception of her situation relative to that of her husband and her other colleagues. *The presence of her husband as a standard for comparison is inescapable, and generally this comparison is negative for the wife because of the relative subordination of her career* (italics added). Although the wife achieves more than women who are not in a professional pair, she achieves less than her most salient comparison, her husband.
>
> Why does the professional pair choose this particular resolution? It seems, in part, that it represents a recognition of past and present differences in professional opportunities afforded men and women, coupled with the different expectations of them in society. In this sense the "easy" road has been chosen, a decision that serves to support and maintain the stereotypes to which it was perceived to be a necessary or rational response (Bryson et al., 1976).

The Bryson et al. study, along with the findings of Garland (1972) and Paloma (1972), document the potential for felt inequity that falls upon the wife in a dual-career marriage. Why have women (and their husbands) been so willing in the past seemingly to accept this situation and generally to deny marital conflict stemming from it? Bryson et al. point to sex-role stereotyping as a partial answer. But they do not elaborate what aspects of sex-role conditioning, in particular, contribute to this. The answer may lie in early learned expectations on the woman's part to accept a subordinate role in society. Much of her experience in her family of origin is likely to involve perceiving her mother acting in an overtly deferential manner to her father. This would be true even if her mother had a career (which is often the case, as noted by Bebbington, 1973). Thus, the pattern in the lives of husband and wife psychologists studied by Bryson et al. essentially may repeat the learned pattern from their families of origin in regard to the wife's acceptance of a subordinate role. However, social changes are occurring along these lines. It is prehaps not surprising that a study of psychologists was among the first writings to elaborate empirically the true feelings married career women have about this state of affairs. Given their professional training, with its emphasis on sensitivity to feelings, at least for some members of the study sample, such women may be more likely to admit to and express conflictual feelings directly, instead of denying them.

More and more women in dual-career marriages seem destined to face and deal forthrightly with the perceived inequity inherent in a subordinate interpersonal role. As this happens, dual-career marriage is likely to be strained and more open conflict engendered. The Women's Liberation Movement (WLM) will be seen as either an ally or a provocateur in this process. The WLM can provide much support and justification for individuals wanting to change perceived inequities. It is likely to be harder and harder for a woman (and her husband) to accept the current state of affairs. In addition, affirmative action programs and other efforts to ameliorate sex discrimination should open up the career opportunities for women. This will hopefully increase felt job satisfaction in the future. All of these social changes may or may not lead to a more equitable division of domestic and child-care responsibilities.

In many ways, the present period may be the time of greatest felt conflict. Consciousness has been raised and yet institutional change lags. Couples are likely to feel and give vent to their frustrations, but find solutions are not at hand. As a result of this process, the marriage is likely to show strain. Dual-career couples seen in marital therapy are often more acutely aware not only of competitive feelings, and their impact on the relationship, but also of other seminal dual-career marital conflicts.

Berman, Sacks and Lief (1975) discuss a particular type of conflict which can arise in a "two-professional" marriage. They note that women professionals have a higher divorce rate than women in general (Rosow and Rose, 1972). Women professionals are likely to marry professional men. For example, 80% of women physicians marry physicians or other professional men (Berman et al., 1975). Given these facts, the authors reasoned that a two-professional marriage is one with a high degree of risk.

Berman et al. describe a common pattern of conflict seen in dual-career couples who met and married during their period of professional training. They begin to feel dissatisfaction with the relationship early in their postschooling professional years and seek marital therapy. Because of similar educational levels and professional aspirations, such individuals *overtly* report that they feel equal to one another. However, Berman et al. state:

> Our clinical impressions lead us to believe that underlying the overt illusion of an equal relationship is a covert traditional stance, that is, a superior, strong male and a more helpless, dependent female. This early covert "contract" tends to result from the wife's early (socially deficient) self image, her underlying needs and her cultural assumptions, and is supported by the underlying expectations of the man. Crucially, these are usually subliminal or unconscious, hidden from both partners. (Berman, Sacks and Lief, 1975, p. 246)

This state of affairs generally holds until the wife acquires an economically productive professional position, at which point her self-concept often changes rapidly in a positive direction. This could be facilitative for growth in the marriage except for the fact that, at or about the same time, Berman et al. note:

> Her opinion of her husband shifts, so that he is now no longer seen (as formerly) as a brilliant student but as a co-worker. The husband's changes in his self-perception and in his appearance to the outside world tend to be far less dramatic than those of his wife. . . . The effect on the marriage of this sudden shift in the husband's apparent status occasioned by both the wife's rise to being a fellow-professional and the husband's apparent drop in "superior" rating is in itself confusing to both, but particularly for the wife. She is still demanding unconsciously that her husband be her superior (her old conditioning) while consciously she expects him to be an equal (her

new ideals). Therefore, particularly and most noticeably in dysfunctional couples, the husband who is now truly an equal, is seen as weak
and less desirable at a time when other men around the wife (colleagues in particular) appear strong and challenging. Her husband,
of course, cannot move either way, because if he attempts to reestablish his superiority, she balks; yet his willingness to accept her
new status tends to be perceived as weakness. The bind each feels
caught in generates increasing frustration and hostility, accentu-
ated by feelings of helplessness because of their inability to understand what is happening. (Berman, Sacks and Lief, 1975, pp. 246–
247).

As a response to this frustration, arguments over small and
seemingly unrelated events increase. One or both partners may
seek out other relationships, sexual or nonsexual, attempting,
thereby, to feel support and justification for their marital dissatisfactions. The husband may voice, for the first time, the wish for a
"traditional" wife, one who would be happy staying at home and
raising children. This, of course, runs counter to the wishes of his
spouse, who is feeling self-esteem enhancement from her professional endeavors. A power struggle around the issue of control
ensues and can eventually lead to divorce, particularly if the
couple does not seek professional help.

Berman et al. relate their findings to the increasing literature
on the developmental stages of adult life. The career woman, in
particular, is seen as often having a growth spurt in the few years
following the completion of her professional training. They note,
"As she begins to receive more external validation of her
achievements as a professional and as a female, and then returns
home to a boring, traditional, or already conflicted relationship,
she begins to feel more and more that she can 'go it alone' " (p.
250). The husband is often more interested in settling down and
finding stability in the marriage. Thus, the wife's rapid advancement can result in the perception of differential growth rates and
changing expectations, leading to conflict.

One of the reasons postulated for the increase in breakdown
of dual-professional marriage is that no longer do career women
customarily take time out from their careers to create a comfortable home for their spouses and/or to have children, with the
expectation of resuming work when the children reach school
age. The prior, customary pattern mirrored more closely traditional marital expectations and avoided some of the circum-

stances which can lead to the type of differential growth conflict, on the part of the wife, described by Berman et al. The traditional pattern, however, can result in conflicts of a different sort, as the woman sees her husband's career advancing while hers remains dormant and she begins to resent the facilitations of his accomplishments as a result of her career "sacrifices."

The "two-professional syndrome" described by Berman et al. is a familiar one to marital therapists. However, conflict can occur at many points throughout the dual-career marital life cycle. Wherever there is differential growth on the part of the spouses, a period of vulnerability to crisis can occur. Healthy marriages have the flexibility to cope with the ebb and flow of each partner's life, achieving new understandings and adjustments where necessary. The Berman et al. paper represents an attempt to document the origin and type of crisis faced by dual-career couples at one particular time in their marriage. Hopefully, future writers will expand this type of formulation to cover other potential dual-career marital crisis points, e.g., when the youngest child leaves home and when retirement is imminent for one or both spouses, to mention only a few.

In an attempt to formulate a more general conceptualization of conflict in dual-career marriage, Rapoport and Rapoport (1971) refer to "identity tension lines" for each spouse. This concept denotes the degree that each individual can transcend his or her social role conditioning, in regard to taking on tasks that have been traditionally associated with the spouse of the opposite gender. The phenomenon can be understood also from a systems theory framework. In this sense, "tension lines" serve to keep the system balanced in regard to task preferences and comfortable assumed role behaviors. A request by one spouse for the other to do more than he or she feels comfortable doing upsets the balance in the system and produces conflict. Renegotiation of a new, mutually agreed-upon task and role division schedule (changing the system as a whole) or a return to the previous way of doing things is required to rebalance the system. For example, the husband has a tension line in regard to how much of the domestic and child-care tasks he can assume and feel the division of labor in the relationship to be equitable. Also, there is often a tension line set up in regard to whether he can tolerate his wife earning a higher income than his own.

From the wife's perspective, she may have a tension line in terms of how much time and effort she can put into her job without feeling neglect of perceived familial responsibilities. Or she may feel tension in the area of how much she can accept the constraints and benefits of success and advancement in her occupational field (all the above examples are from Rapoport and Rapoport, 1975).

The Rapoports feel that "working on tension lines seems . . . at this point in history to be a crucial element in achieving sustained and equitable change" (1975, p. 428). However, tension lines appear to be a product of sex-role socialization and should slowly change and diminish in the future, given less rigid gender-role conditioning. Many present-day *couples* feel concern and stress in the same individual conflict areas noted above. For example, *both* husband and wife often question how far they can go in terms of occupational achievement (and its accompanying responsibilities) without sacrificing family life. Thus, it seems that the couple may have a relationship tension line in certain areas, which can transcend individual conflicts and individual equity concerns.

In summary, generic dual-career marital conflicts elaborated in the studies reviewed so far in this chapter have generally been related to the areas of (a) felt competition between the spouses, (b) distribution of power in the marriage, and (c) marital and family support structure. A further elaboration of the character of these generic conflict areas is provided below.

COMPETITION BETWEEN SPOUSES

Although denied by many, if not most, dual-career couples, competitive feelings related to each other's careers are natural and inevitable. From a psychological standpoint, it seems better to face competitive feelings directly than to have them expressed indirectly, e.g., in emotional and affectional withdrawal from the marital relationship.

The likelihood of felt competitiveness with one's spouse is heightened because of the type of individuals who adopt a dual-career marital life-style. As elaborated in Chapter 4, both spouses generally have high achievement needs. Their educational history is typically one of successful competition through intellectual competence and/or hard work. *However, the need to feel competitive is not necessarily based on having to win or to beat one another down.* It can be related to putting one's abilities to the test and feeling as if one has "come through."

The potential for feeling competitive with one's spouse is also strongly related to equity or fairness considerations. Given past demonstrated abilities and prior educational or career achievements, it is natural to assess oneself, at least periodically, in terms of "how am I doing" vis-à-vis peers, including one's spouse. If the assessment results in perceived inequity, particularly in comparison with one's marital partner, a state of conflict is commonly engendered.

Given the traditional differential career patterning of men and women, as elaborated by Garland (1972), Paloma (1972), Berman et al. (1975) and Bryson et al. (1976), the resolution of such perceived conflict is more than likely to be in the wife's disfavor. She has customarily been expected to make certain career sacrifices while her husband advances, e.g., to delay or slow down her career when the children are young, to find a job where her husband locates or to accept a less prestigious position as the result of nepotism rules. Although this may have been a personally and mutually agreed-upon choice and, even if there are many rewards and positive benefits of the decision—e.g., in having and raising children—for many career women the sum total of gains and losses simply does not balance out fairly.

Whenever she must assess the results of these sacrifices in terms of her career achievements, conflictual and competitive feelings and resentments may result. Only by restructuring such an assessment to include primarily noncareer areas—e.g., her capabilities as a mother, her social accomplishments, and/or the material benefits gained from her husband's accomplishments—can many married career women avoid conflictual feelings. Given the time and effort required for career preparation, allowing her own career a prominent position in this assessment can usually not be put off for long. Facing the feelings of inequity and career disadvantage that result can be a painful process and resorting to denial of competitive feelings seems to be an easier, if only temporary, solution. A common result, when competitive feelings can no longer be denied, is for the dual-career wife to show her resentment over career inequities indirectly, usually to the detriment of the marriage and at the expense of felt personal happiness. A case study will illustrate this process:

Case #9. Jan, age 33, and Eric, age 34, have been married for ten years and have two children, Tommy, age 8, and Beth, age 6. Both spouses came from affluent families, who were nonetheless governed by a strong work ethic. Eric was the oldest of three brothers and the most favored. His father was president of a manufacturing company and his mother, a college graduate, had not pursued a career but was prominent in social and civic affairs. Jan's mother had worked as a nurse before Jan was born. However, she stopped working once Jan arrived, and had not resumed her career even though Jan and her younger brother were now grown. Her father was a physician and her memories of him seemed generally positive, though she remembers feeling at times "like his patients had first call on his attention." Eric was intellectually precocious and showed a special interest in science, which was fostered by both parents. He progressed rapidly and easily through school, completing his doctorate in a physical science area. After two postdoctoral years, at age 28, he began as an assistant professor at a prestigious university. Four years later he was awarded tenure (considered by the institution to be a rare, "early" promotion), based on many hours of research in his lab, and the resultant series of creative, nationally recognized publications.

Eric in many ways epitomized the successful academic. He was giving to his students and active in departmental affairs, while still devoting much time (including many weekends) to his research. The latter was heavily supported by federal grant funds, for which he had competed successfully. In the eyes of colleagues and friends, Eric's family was supportive and satisfying. Jan was characterized by others as "understanding" and "tolerant" of the long hours needed by Eric for his work. Tommy and Beth were apparently happy and well adjusted children, benefiting from their membership in what a friend described (with mild envy) as "the All-American family."

At age 33, when he was apparently at the height of his academic career, Eric resigned his professorship and took a research and administrative job with the government, uprooting his family and leaving behind surprised friends and shocked colleagues. Only at this point did others realize that the outside presentation of this family may have masked strong underlying negative affect. Beneath the surface lay resentment and bitterness, particularly on Jan's part, and increasingly for Tommy and Beth, who wondered at times, *Why does Daddy work so much?*

Forgotten by others (and by Eric himself during much of their marriage) were Jan's career plans. Her initial ambivalence surrounding the acceptance of a traditional marital contract eventually was tipped in a negative direction. While taking much pride in (and secret credit for) many of Eric's accomplishments, she began to feel like an appendage of her husband and, increasingly, a vestigial one, especially as she was forced to acknowledge Tommy and Beth's growing independence.

Jan had begun graduate work after her marriage and had completed two years of study in biological science. She was writing her master's thesis at the time they left to begin Eric's academic position. She had intended to resume her studies in the new location but became pregnant with Tommy shortly after her arrival and decided to postpone the completion of her graduate work. She began again six years later (when Beth was 3), with Eric's verbal support, but without much help on his part in regard to sharing domestic responsibilities. By using a combination of school, day-care, and outside help she was able to resume her studies on a nearly full-time basis and (after much struggle, fortitude and some "retreading" of basic knowledge) had passed her preliminary exams and begun work on her dissertation. At this point, Eric decided to resign his academic position.

The couple had talked things over and agreed that the career opportunities for Jan would be better in a different location. She also "did not want to live in Eric's shadow" by pursuing a possible academic appointment at "his university." She wished to begin her delayed career on her own. Throughout her family background ran a strong theme of stubborn independence that facilitated her going back to school after a six-year absence. Having outside (family) income made it easier to arrange a support system with Eric's minimal help; however, she felt an undercurrent of resentment over how their contract had facilitated his career achievements at the expense of her own.

When they entered therapy, neither was aware initially that the resentment and bitterness she felt toward him (which led to their seeking counseling) was based partly on *competitive* feelings. She said, "I always thought a husband and wife should help each other, not compete with one another." When asked whether her expectations at the time they were married in regard to her having a career (the implicit contract) had been met, she said, "For a while I thought so. I mean it was okay for Eric to go ahead with his job; he was doing so well, you know. But, if you're asking me whether I feel it's been fair or not, knowing what I know now, I'd have to say no. But, you know, I didn't realize that until recently." (That, indeed, was what the therapist was asking, and Jan's answer read like a line straight from a treatise on equity theory.) Eric registered mild surprise at her answer, saying: "Well, I thought it was fine with Jan if I went ahead and worked hard. She seemed happy that I was doing well. She did ask me to help some at home and I said, 'It's okay to hire Fran' (the maid and cleaning lady). I'm honestly not sure where all her anger at me is coming from. I mean, I want her to be happy with her life, too." Jan's eyebrows lifted at the patronizing aspect of Eric's comment, but she said nothing.

Eventually, therapy helped them to see that her (their) competitive feelings were natural, given the situation and circumstances of their lives. Jan began to state her expectations of Eric more clearly in regard to the temporal and task support she expected. He felt at a plateau in his career and began to see that, in his single-minded pursuit up the academic ladder, he was leaving his family (and perhaps himself) behind emotionally. An attractive aspect of the government position involved the greater regularity of advancement offered and the reduced degree of peer competitiveness. The offer came at the right time psychologically and he decided to accept.

Eric did not resent or attempt to deny Jan's competitive feelings, and seemed genuinely (if occasionally patronizingly) to understand her wish to achieve career success. Fortunately, he was flexible and open to changing his job and life-style in order to help facilitate Jan's career. If this hadn't happened, she would have had to modify her career plans or ultimately perhaps initiate a divorce, the latter being an increasingly common response to spouse inflexibility and resistance to change in the direction of greater relationship equity.

In summary, most dual-career couples must face natural and probably inevitable competitive feelings directly and honestly. One spouse's seeking to win a "prize" in this competition, at the expense of the other, is likely to be disruptive to marital harmony. Rather, in a healthy state of competition, *both* partners are motivated by the goals of career success and personal and marital fulfillment. The therapist can help the couple achieve these goals by bringing competitive feelings out in the open, where they can be expressed forthrightly and dealt with directly. The therapeutic process in this regard is elaborated in Chapter 8.

POWER CONFLICTS IN DUAL-CAREER MARRIAGE

Issues regarding the distribution of power in marital relationships have been frequently discussed in the marital therapy literature. Focusing on power dynamics is important in the clinical assessment of marital conflicts. Several present-day writers have elaborated on the multidimensional nature of the concept of power.

Safilios-Rothschild (1976) indicates nine different types of power that can be present in a marital relationship. One of these, "resource power," is ascribed to a person based on educational or occupational achievements. By virtue of such attainments, the individual can control certain scarce, desirable resources (e.g., income) necessary for the functioning of the relationship. In traditional marriage, the husband generally has a greater degree of resource power than the wife. (Most systems theorists, however, believe that in a continuing relationship there is an even distribution of overall power between the family members. In a traditional marital relationship, the husband's greater resource power is balanced commonly by the wife's greater "influence" power, i.e., gaining a certain amount of control in a relationship by working "behind the scenes," often using nonverbal, sexual, and emotional techniques to achieve desired ends.)

Dual-career marriage differs from traditional marriage in that both partners generally have a high degree of resource power. Thus, the wife is not totally dependent upon her husband for financial support. One of the important implications of this is that she does not have to stay in an unsatisfying marriage purely for financial reasons. She (or he) can choose to stay or to leave with *both* alternatives as viable financial options. This very fact alters dramatically the power relationship in dual-career couples, compared with traditionally married spouses. It is perhaps a mixed blessing. Depending on one's viewpoint, having a true choice may result in less motivation for the couple to work on an unproductive relationship, preferring instead to leave. Or, conversely, it may promote a stronger relationship by enabling the couple to stay together because they *want* to, not because they *have* to.

Many marital therapists (including the author) believe the perception by the spouses of a real choice results generally in a positive motivational force, leading couples to work on improving their marriage. They often prefer this to the alternative of sinking back into routine and stagnation, sadly accepting that "he (she) is never going to change, so why make the effort?"

There is a strong impetus for contemporary dual-career couples to favor an egalitarian ethic as their dominant philosophy of marriage (Fogarty, Rapoport and Rapoport, 1971; Rapoport and Rapoport, 1975). This is potentiated by having similar levels of educational attainment and occupational status. However, old ideas and conditioned behaviors fade slowly, and conflict can result from differing husband–wife values and beliefs. For example, a husband may feel generally comfortable with his wife's working until in the midst of a host of job demands, she begins to neglect her share of household duties. At this point, he may wish he had married a full-time "homemaker" (like his mother) instead of a career woman. Voicing his expectations in this regard is likely to set the stage for an argument or, at the very least, guilt feelings on the wife's part.

Many of the conflicts which result from such value clashes have strong power themes, as defined in terms of which spouse can exert greater influence over the other in the making of important decisions. This is perhaps epitomized for dual-career couples when one spouse has been offered a job in a particular location and the other spouse does not have an offer of comparable attractiveness. Traditionally, the wife was expected to go where her husband could get a job. Although dual-career couples report some weight having been given to the wife's career possibilities when choosing a job location (Garland, 1972; Holmstrom, 1972; Wallston, Foster and Berger, 1978; Weingarten, 1978), generally the ultimate decision tends to be made in favor of the husband. This is particularly true in those dual-career marriages where the wife has been expected (and has agreed) to modify her occupational behavior while the children are young, either interrupting her career or "slowing down" by working less than full time.

Other possible and perhaps more equitable solutions to the dilemma posed by differential job availability include both spouses sharing a single job (particularly if both are in the same career field) or taking jobs in different locations (with one spouse commuting back and forth so the couple can be together, at least on weekends). Unfortunately, the inflexibility of the contemporary occupational structure often precludes innovative solutions such as job sharing, flexible starting and stopping times, or part-time work for both spouses (Holmstrom, 1972). This is elaborated in Chapter 10.

As was previously discussed regarding competitive feelings, a common by-product of unresolved marital power conflicts is felt alienation and emotional withdrawal from the relationship. In traditional marriage, a wife who feels dominated, subjugated and oppressed by her husband often resorts to "evening the score" through controlling her sexual availability and participation. These behaviors are seen in dual-career couples, e.g., where their pattern of decreased intimacy becomes an accurate barometer of a spouse's feeling "one-down" to his or her partner in regard to an inequitable distribution of decision-making and influence in the marriage. As noted in Chapter 4, an alternative response to felt dual-career marital unhappiness is for each spouse to withdraw from the marriage into his or her job, putting greater energy into an aspect of one's life where there is greater felt control and determination. Such diversion of effort usually occurs ultimately at the expense of felt intimacy and marital satisfaction. A case study presented below illustrates some of the power conflicts typically seen in dual-career marriage.

Case #10. Don and Sally, both 28, have been married for two years and have no children. They are completing postdoctoral training in the same field of applied science. They attended graduate school together and were married during the time both were working on their dissertations. Sally completed her doctorate near the beginning of her first postdoctoral year and Don finished later the same year. They began to look for jobs during the latter half of their second postdoctoral year. Although they were in the same field, they had generally not felt competitive conflicts during graduate school. Indeed, both perceived a synergistic effect in their relationship, in terms of each helping the other to do well,

82

e.g., by dividing up the readings for their preliminary exams and then sharing notes. They felt pleased and fortunate to have received postdoctoral offers at the same institution.

Don came from a scholarly family. His father was a professor in the humanities at a large public university and his mother was a commercial artist. He had a sister two years younger, who was currently doing graduate work in education. Don was close to his father and knew from a fairly early age that "I was probably going to be a professor of something or other one of these days."

Although his father had been generally relaxed in regard to his (verbally communicated) aspirations for Don, his mother more directly articulated that she expected him "to do well at whatever you do." Don perceived, at least at times, that her basic caring for him seemed contingent on his continued achievement. This led to feelings of ambivalence toward his mother and a desire to rebel against her performance expectations. He handled these rebellious feelings during adolescence by withholding detailed information from his mother in regard to school activities (particularly awards he had won) and his social life ("which was not extensive, but at least Mom didn't know about it"). He "goofed around" in high school but "caught fire" during his sophomore year in college when a professor in his field-to-be took an interest in him and offered gentle, nurturant praise and support, much like that accorded by Don's father. Graduate school had gone well, although Don was aware of the degree to which he needed "strokes" from others (particularly male professors) to sustain his interest and motivation.

Socially, Don began dating more frequently when he went to college, joined a "fringe" fraternity and had a couple of serious relationships with women during his undergraduate years, each of which ended when one or the other of the participants left school. He started dating Sally in the middle of his second year of graduate work, after having known her on a friendship basis in several courses they had taken.

Sally was an excellent student, who was, nonetheless, in Don's words, "not showy about her knowledge. She got a lot of good feedback from her professors. She handled that in a quiet way which I liked. We had lots of interesting discussions and I liked the way her mind worked. But we had fun, too, it wasn't just an intellectual relationship. I felt as if I was a little ahead of Sally socially, and a little more comfortable with people. I felt like I could help make things easier for her there, if you know what I mean." The inference was that Don's greater social adroitness balanced Sally's more evident intellectual capability and enabled each to feel as if they brought something to the relationship, while not perceiving the other's differential capabilities as psychologically threatening.

Sally came from a family of lower socioeconomic means than Don's. Her father died suddenly during her last year in high school. He was employed as a skilled craftsman, believed in hard work and conveyed the wish to his children that they "do better than I did." That meant an emphasis on getting a good education for Sally and her two younger brothers, and she at least had not resisted these expectations. Her mother was a strong and nurturant woman, who went to work in a factory after her husband died, although she had not been employed outside the home during her marriage.

Sally described herself as a "good girl, in general," who felt loved by both parents, but had felt closer to her father. "I could identify with some of his struggles in life. I mean, I really believed he wanted me to have it better. He seemed to care about me and what happened to me." Her father's support was reinforced by several teachers (male and female) who recognized Sally's intellectual potential at an early age and encouraged her development along these lines. Her father's unexpected death left her shaken but resolute. "I felt like he wanted me to go on in school, as far as I could. It helped when Mom took over and went to work. For a while I thought I might have to get a job and not go to college right away."

Socially, Sally started dating midway through high school, but she had never had a really serious relationship before her marriage to Don. "Just a couple of summer things, when I was a camp counselor, but they didn't last past September." She was generally comfortable socially in dating relationships ("It helped to have brothers") but felt that pursuing an education was more important than getting married ("I'm not sure I'd want Mother's life"). Eventually, she was attracted to Don "because he seemed to have similar goals and he could appreciate where my head was . . . about finishing grad school and starting in on a career."

Don and Sally's relationship had generally been an easy and comfortable one through the end of their first year of marriage. They made friends with two other couples who enjoyed outdoor activities (camping, cycling, etc.). It was not until they began in their second year of marriage to talk about getting jobs that a gradual uncomfortableness started to creep into their relationship. Don seemed aware that the character of the job market, already favorable to women professionals, could well work in Sally's favor (and "against" him). Partly to avoid direct competition, they decided to look for somewhat different jobs, Don in academia, Sally in industry or government. This was consistent with his long-standing wish to be a professor and her relative disinterest in teaching.

Because of the pseudomutual character of their relationship (i.e., the need to exaggerate felt compatibility in order to avoid facing conflict directly), Don could not tell Sally about his fear that she was going to get a better job. He entered therapy because of his own troubled feelings along these lines and the resultant felt breakdown in marital communication. The therapist suggested that Sally be involved in therapy, too, and Don reluctantly agreed to include her for the second and subsequent sessions.

Part of Don's fears had to do with projected expectations that Sally would lose respect for him if he did not secure a job of comparable status to her own position. From a psychodynamic standpoint, this harked back to his struggle with his mother around perceived demands that he do well (or risk her rejection). True to old patterns, he rebelled against these projected expectations by delaying his job search until late in his academic year and by not going to the national convention, where young professionals in his field typically learned about and interviewed for prospective jobs. He also had dragged out the completion of his dissertation, almost carrying through a self-fulfilled prophecy, since he knew that if he had not completed his doctorate he would be unable to enter academia at the higher status position of assistant professor (and would be relegated instead to the title of "instructor"). Sally did not help in regard to Don's troubles. She went ahead with her job search and, although she noticed a decline in their communication, was overtly not cognizant of the underlying competitive power struggle. In part, she did not realize what was going on because Don could not talk about it, and thus a vicious circle was perpetuated.

As if to follow the script, Sally was offered a prestigious job in a city they both felt to be a desirable place to live. Don felt "glad for her," but increasingly ambivalent about their relationship. Sexual activities, which had not been the most satisfying aspect of their marriage, due largely to both partners' relative inexperience, began to decline in frequency and intimacy. Realizing that he could keep silent no longer, Don began to express his underlying feelings, somewhat to Sally's surprise. She said, "Well, I never knew that side of him. I always felt Don would get a good job—he's done well and he's from a good school, you know." In therapy, Sally began to realize that she had become the unanticipated third party in a now triangulated ambivalent relationship between Don and his mother.

The couple resolved that Sally should take the job and that Don would go along and look for a position there, even if it meant a year for him without a professional appointment. At the last minute, following a period of budgetary delays, an assistant professorship became available at a university in the vicinity of where they would be living. Fortunately, Don had interviewed a short time earlier with the head of the department and things had gone well. A second visit and series of interviews with other department members was arranged quickly and Don was ultimately offered the position, which he accepted.

Although things were resolved satisfactorily for Don and Sally, the pseudomutuality which had characterized their relationship, serving as a dyadic defense against facing conflict, could (perhaps fortunately) no longer be maintained. They both realized that power issues had to be faced directly, if a satisfying level of verbal and physical communication was to be maintained. Don saw in her (and others) the potential for "pushing my Mom button." Sally realized that an unanticipated by-product of the general harmony which had characterized her family life was that it left her ill prepared to face the inevitable and even normative conflict likely to occur periodically in her marriage.

In summary, power conflicts, defined in terms of which spouse exerts a preferential influence over decision making in a dual-career marriage, often result paradoxically from the relatively greater freedom that such couples (compared to individuals in a traditional marriage) have in terms of choosing whether or not they will stay together. The ability of each to support himself or herself on a financially independent basis brings with it the possibility of leaving a dysfunctional relationship without the need to depend on another person for financial support. Having a choice also means that underlying power struggles may be brought into open, direct conflict (e.g., when the couple must decide which partner gets job location preference) instead of being waged covertly. Handling such conflicts directly can avoid their displacement onto other areas of the couple's interaction, most commonly, their sexual relationship. The overt character of the power struggle results in part from *both* partners in dual-career marriages having a high degree of "resource power" (Safilios-Rothschild, 1976) by virtue of their educational attainments and occupational status and, therefore, having a high potential for influencing decision making in the relationship.

CONFLICTS ASSOCIATED WITH THE MARITAL SUPPORT STRUCTURE

Most dual-career couples find it impossible to function without outside help for domestic tasks. This is particularly the case when a couple has children. In the not too distant past, as elaborated in the Paloma (1972) study, a career woman was expected to have two jobs—three if there were children involved—to her husband's one. She could work outside the home, but it was expected that this would be in addition to her job as "full-time" housekeeper and mother. This is still the pattern in many dual-worker families today, and it is also the situation in many other countries for couples where both spouses work, e.g., in Russia (noted in Rapoport and Rapoport, 1975).

One outcome of this uneven distribution of domestic tasks is that the wife often feels minimal time and energy left over for the marital relationship. Traditionally, women have assumed perhaps too readily a disproportionate share of domestic responsibility, partly as a result of prior social conditioning and in order to avoid feeling guilt over their career and what it "took away" from family life. Fortunately for the psychological growth aspects of dual-career marriage, this prior pattern is changing. Career women are demanding and getting help with domestic duties, both from their spouses and from outside employees. Indeed, a good part of the couples' increased earnings as a result of dual employment is most likely to go toward paying for support services (St. John-Parsons, 1978).

87

Conflicts in the support system area revolve around (a) how much outside help is really necessary (translation: "How much of our income do we have to pay out to other people?"), and (b) what happens when the support structure (inevitably) breaks down. Both spouses in a dual-career marriage may feel as if they are "buying out" of domestic responsibilities by contracting for outside help. To a certain extent, this is true. However, any implicit understanding along these lines is seriously tested when the support system does not come through and the partners must decide who will assume the domestic and/or child-care responsibilities which revert back to them. This is likely to happen either when one of the parties, the children or the help is sick, or during times of "turnover" (for many couples, it seems as if someone whom you have come to rely upon is always leaving or is about to leave).

An essential requirement for most dual-career couples, particularly if they have children, is an adequate "backup" system. This consists of a second group of individuals the couple can turn to for help when the primary support system breaks down. If backup is not available, the spouses must grapple with the question of "who can stay home and take care of this?" Such questions are difficult because they become easily translated into "whose job is more important?" Each partner is likely to feel that the other should be flexible and conciliatory at such times. If one spouse is always making the sacrifice, sooner or later a felt inequity will result and eventually lead to greater problems for the couple. In general, dual-career spouses try to avoid testing directly the issue of whose job is more important. The answer, of course, is that this is really a nonquestion; both careers are important, and each is certainly more important for the individual and, indirectly, for the relationship than unimportant.

Ideally, the responsibility for *arranging* the support structure should be shared by the partners. If not, it is too easy to blame the spouse who did the arranging. Usually, this means husband blames wife. The accusation generally has undertones of "you are a poor housekeeper (or mother)," and this can play into the wife's career ambivalence and role strain. She resents the implication but, often out of guilt and self-questioning (in regard to whether she is doing the "right thing" by working), cannot "call" her husband on it. An outcome of this process is that issues regarding the support system once again become "her problem" rather than "our problem." If she redoubles her efforts or attempts to do both partners' share, it is likely to be at the temporal and/or emotional expense of the relationship.

The marital therapist's efforts in regard to the couple's support system often involve helping them to keep a variety of factors (money, time, individuals) in balance. It is essential for the couple to discuss and negotiate openly and directly any expectations of shared responsibility for arranging and maintaining the support structure. Many of these difficulties have not and perhaps could not have been anticipated at the beginning of the couple's relationship. Therefore, some help with revising the marital contract is usually in order. The next three chapters will discuss these and other psychotherapeutic considerations in dealing with dual-career couples.

·7·

Therapy with Dual-Career Couples: General Considerations

How Marital Therapy Differs from Other Psychotherapeutic Modalities

In general, the psychotherapeutic skills helpful in working with any individual (or couple) are applicable to dealing with individuals in dual-career marriages. The therapist needs to have good rapport and relationship establishing skills, a high capacity for empathic understanding and an appreciation for the range and individualized nature of adaptable human behavior. Beyond these generic considerations, therapists who work with dual-career couples need to be aware of certain particular aspects and limitations of marital therapy as a treatment modality. There are specific ways in which marital therapy differs from individual therapy, in particular, as well as from other treatment forms, such as group therapy. The author's bias and, indeed, the empirical findings on marital therapy outcome, indicate that conjoint treatment of husband and wife is the most effective way to treat marital problems (Gurman and Kniskern, 1978). Separate treatment of husband and/or wife, while potentially facilitative of *individual* growth, does not reliably lead to needed *marital* change. From a systems framework, this lack of a positive marital outcome can be understood in terms of the need for the marital system to remain in balance. Change by one partner upsets the balance and often results in an attempt by the other partner to bring the system back into its original homeostasis (Steinglass, 1978). When both partners are in treatment, there is hopefully a mutual desire to change and, in the process, to evolve a new, stable system of interaction. The greater efficiency of conjoint treatment accounts.

90

in large part, for the strong preference of this therapeutic format among marital therapists.

The therapist is reminded continually that the strongest relationship bonding in the marital therapy situation is likely to be, and to remain, that between the spouses. This holds even when one is working with a separated and/or divorcing couple. The strength of interspouse relationship bonding serves to limit the degree of influence the therapist can have in helping the couple to change their behavior. It also contrasts with the nature and dynamics of most individual therapy and, to a lesser extent, with group therapy, where the strong transference bonding between therapist and patient(s) often permits the therapist to have a good deal of leverage in facilitating personality change. The individual or group therapist may thus become (for a while) the most important "other" in that individual's life. This is rarely the case in marital therapy, where the spouse, for better or worse, is and is likely to continue to be, the most important other.

This single limitation on the degree of the marital therapist's influence leads to a variety of other general implications for working with couples. One of these is the high degree of resistance to change that tends to characterize marital therapy. Couples have, by definition, a history of interaction with one another and they have developed typically a system that is protective against outside influence. Indeed, the development of consensual dyadic boundaries is necessary for the couple to preserve their relationship against undue external influences. For example, such boundaries set limits on the degree to which relatives and in-laws are permitted to impact on the couple's behavior.

A marriage in which the dyad is unable to demarcate their own territory in this regard is often unable to manifest the growth and change over time characteristic of a dynamic, healthy relationship. The individuals remain developmentally fixated in their families of origin, retaining their major identity vis-à-vis important others as "son" or "daughter," rather than as "husband" or "wife."

As a result of the marital relationship boundaries, the marital therapist often meets strong resistance from the couple at the very beginning of therapy. Unless such resistance can be overcome, therapy is likely to end quickly, with little or no positive benefit. It is important for the therapist to try to work *with* the couple's resistance, rather than *against* it. One way this can be accomplished is to try to discern carefully, early in therapy, what the couple wishes to work on. If there is a discrepancy between the spouses in this regard, the therapist should try to help them clarify a problem area of joint concern and secure the agreement of both partners to begin work on this. This treatment strategy helps the therapist to join together with the couple in a common task, thus promoting a "therapeutic alliance" (Smith and Grunebaum, 1976). The problem area chosen for initial focus may not prove eventually to have been the most important problem area for the couple. It should, however, be an area of serious concern, in order to facilitate the establishing of a working therapeutic alliance.

Typically, the therapist begins treatment with an agenda, comprised largely of his or her knowledge about common patterns of marital dysfunction and the need to assess the couple or family in terms of these varied dimensions. The therapist usually wants to know, for example, how money is managed, how important decisions are made, the relationships to families of origin, sexual behavior patterns and satisfactions, boundaries of the relationship regarding friends and possible other intimates, as well as other marital interaction areas. In this manner, most therapists need some overall picture of the marital and family systems before proceeding with treatment. At the same time, the couple is likely focused on specific problem area(s) that brought them into therapy. They may be tolerant of the therapist's need to explore the larger system picture, but dealing with this may run counter to the urgency of dealing with their specific presenting problems. Thus, the therapist brings in one agenda; the couple or family has a different agenda. The priorities of the two agendas are likely to differ.

The therapist needs to be flexible and to avoid imposing his or her own format or theoretical belief system onto the couple too quickly. Otherwise, initial resistance to the therapist's interventions may be mobilized. The same risk, and caution, applies to all forms of psychotherapeutic treatment. The initial client resistance mobilized, however, is likely to be greater when dealing with couples or families (and, to a lesser extent, with nonfamilial groups). Such individuals are likely to have a more extensive history of alliance with one another than with the therapist, and this can be used to resist the therapist's interventions.

In summary, the couple needs early in therapy to perceive that the therapist is respecting "where they are" and working with their concept of "the problem" right from the beginning of treatment. For dual-career couples, this means that issues regarding the facilitation of their occupational endeavors and/or problems with the marital support structure have a high salience. Therapists who see the spouses' presenting problem(s) as only a "symptom" of deeper, underlying conflicts which form the "real work" of therapy often have difficulty in treating dual-career or other couples. Early interpretation of the couple's presenting problems as mainly "symptomatic" can serve to mobilize strong, dyadic resistance against the therapist. For example, the question, "Why do you feel the need to work when there are small children at home?", directed at the wife in a dual-career marriage, can be counterproductive early in therapy. This particularly true if the therapist's nuance of expression in asking such a question conveys a bias against women working when there are young children in the family. The resultant perceived therapist–client value conflict is likely to engender client resistance.

The above guideline of attending seriously to presenting problems does not mean that the alternative conceptual formulation by the therapist is incorrect; indeed, the presenting marital dysfunction problem(s) may be indicative symptomatically of deeper, underlying individual personality problems. For example, partners who come to therapy complaining of "not having sex often enough" may each have strong, basic fears of intimacy. At some point in couple therapy the latter issue is likely to be addressed and interpreted; however, to begin therapy by interpreting the (albeit mutual) underlying problem as the primary focus often produces a good deal of anxiety and resultant defensiveness. A more productive way to begin therapy, if both spouses agree that infrequency of sexual interaction is an important problem, is to explore the circumstances of and feelings about their sexual relationship, as well as each partner's sexual history (Sager, 1976).

A further implication of the strong, early dyadic resistance commonly seen in marital therapy has to do with the therapist's activity level. In contrast to other forms of therapy, particularly individual treatment, the marital therapist needs generally to be more active within the session. This is especially true early in therapy and is related to the two defining characteristics of marital therapy previously discussed: (a) the main "bonding" in therapy being and remaining that between the spouses, and (b) the high degree of early dyadic resistance to the therapist's interventions.

Given the couple's typically well defined relationship boundaries, the therapist will have to work actively in order to become a meaningful part of the marital system. This is another reason why it is necessary very early in marital therapy to join "with" the couple and establish an effective therapeutic alliance. The partners are capable of collusion against the therapist (and other "outsiders") and usually have a history of some success in this regard. They may regard passive, nondirective behavior on the therapist's part (e.g., the therapist's statement: "I'm just here to listen and try to help") as evidence that they have successfully collaborated to render the therapist ineffective. This does not mean that the therapist actively needs to overpower the couple verbally, leaving them with little time or space for interaction. Instead, the ideal rhythm of treatment early in therapy involves an active give-and-take between the therapist(s) and the couple around commonly agreed-upon area(s) of concern.

In contrast to individual therapy, marital therapy often lasts for a fewer number of total treatment sessions. Gurman and Kniskern (1978) summarize the literature in this regard. Marital therapists report a median of approximately nine treatment sessions per couple in the studies surveyed. Studies of individual psychotherapy indicate a similar median number of treatment sessions in a general outpatient clinic setting. The range for individual therapy, however, is much greater than that for marital therapy, because of a tendency for a greater number of individual cases to be seen for a large number of treatment sessions, particularly in intensive psychotherapy.

There are many possible reasons for the difference between marital and individual therapy in regard to treatment duration. Primary among these is the common experience of spouses eventually "taking over" as therapists for one another, based in part on the modeling done by the therapist. From the marital therapy experience, the partners may acquire certain generic therapeutic skills and modes of relating, e.g., responding empathically to one another, listening more effectively to what each is saying, and providing helpful emotional support. Given two individuals with a meaningful relationship and a sustaining commitment to one another, they can often begin to relate therapeutically, thus feeling less need to be in therapy. When this happens, being able to experience an enhanced meaningful relationship with one's significant other outside of therapy can lead to a desire to terminate the marital therapy sessions. This does not mean that a goal of marital therapy is to make each spouse the other's therapist. Hopefully, improved generic human relationship skills are acquired and, when manifested in interpersonal interaction, such behaviors can have what is usually thought of as therapeutic value.

Since the therapist will likely see couples for a relatively abbreviated time period, it is important that he or she be an active participant, particularly in the early treatment sessions. The fact of such temporal constraints supports the previously elaborated treatment strategy of working with the couple to establish a mutually agreed-upon problem area for beginning therapeutic work.

In summary, a general model of marital therapy is presented which is characterized by: (a) a stronger relationship bonding between the couple than between the therapist and the couple or between the therapist and either spouse, (b) a strong, early dyadic resistance to the therapist's interventions, (c) the need for an agreed-upon definition of what problem(s) are to be worked on early in therapy and therapist respect for the couple's definition in this regard, (d) the need for a higher therapist activity level than is commonly the case in individual treatment, and (e) the likelihood that couple therapy will be short-term therapy, with fewer expected treatment sessions than is often true of individual therapy. The focus has been on those generic aspects of marital therapy likely to characterize the treatment, regardless of the therapist's theoretical orientation. In other words, whatever approach is utilized needs to take into account the above facets of marital therapy.

THE THERAPIST'S ATTITUDES AND BIASES

Many practitioners of marriage counseling and marital therapy have until recently been biased in the direction of preserving "traditional" marriage (Rice and Rice, 1977). This is not surprising, in that not only did most professionals in the field grow up in families characterized by a traditional marital "style," but also they have more likely than not chosen this pattern for their own marriage. Compounding the above is the fact that a majority of the practitioners are male and may be limited in their receptiveness to alternative female marital and occupational role choices. Until recently, the goal of marital therapy, agreed upon by the couple and the therapist, has frequently been to help the spouses adjust more comfortably to the parameters and limitations of traditional marriage. This therapeutic objective has been aided by the ready sociocultural support for traditional marriage.

As long as the couple themselves feel comfortable with the roles and expectations of traditional marriage, there is little problem as a result of any therapist biases along these lines. However, such a therapist will probably find himself or herself in conflict with certain values and preferences of a dual-career couple. For the latter individuals, a good deal of the conflict which led them to seek marital help is commonly tied in with traditional marital role expectations and behaviors. Unless the therapist is sensitive to and open regarding the parameters of this alternative marital lifestyle, the couple is likely to perceive rather quickly a value discrepancy between themselves and the therapist.

A common occurrence in this situation is for the (usually male) therapist to reinforce subtly the husband's ambivalence regarding the wife's career and the demands and expectations it has placed on him. When the wife senses that this is happening in the therapy situation, she is likely to feel outnumbered and without a perceived "ally" for her viewpoint. The covert husband–therapist collusion can upset the working balance between the couple and the therapist. The wife's frequent response to such a situation is to withdraw emotionally, thus undermining therapeutic progress. If the couple is working with a female therapist, a similar potential exists for perceived value discrepancy and resultant collusion between the therapist and the wife that can be disruptive of the therapeutic alliance. In this case, the husband will perceive the therapist to be strongly on the side of his wife. Not feeling supported in his viewpoint, he is likely to react defensively, e.g., by either withdrawing from therapy or subtly attacking the credibility and/or competence of the therapist.

The therapist who treats dual-career couples must honestly examine any biases he or she has regarding personal attitudes toward and feelings about this life-style. The task may be easier for a woman therapist who, by virtue of having a career herself, may be more easily attuned to the endemic problems faced by dual-career couples. However, the woman therapist's own marital and/or familial experiences may have left her with certain biases and unresolved conflicts that limit her therapeutic effectiveness. Discomfort with her own professional role (e.g., feelings about being a social worker in a strongly hierarchical professional mental health setting, which gives higher status to individuals addressed as "doctor") or unsureness about whether she is neglecting her own family by having a career, if not worked through, can limit therapeutic effectiveness. Similar examples could, of course, be given for male therapists. A more reliable format for countering the potential effect of such biases is to have male and female professional co-therapists. While certainly not a panacea, two therapists who are able to model an equitable relationship for the couple may have an advantage in overcoming some of the biases faced by many therapists who treat dual-career couples. Further advantages and limitations of having co-therapists are discussed in Chapter 9.

IMPLICATIONS OF PERSONALITY "STYLE"

In Chapter 4, common personality patterns and behaviors characteristic of dual-career marital partners were elaborated. Such individuals were described as manifesting perfectionism and high motivation for achievement. They were seen as often having difficulty maintaining self-esteem in the absence of external reinforcement and as somewhat reluctant to make interpersonal commitments, since these usually lack a guarantee of success. One would expect such personality factors to impact on the marital therapy relationship and, indeed, this is the case.

Individuals who enter dual-career marriages are usually intelligent, verbal persons who solve problems predominantly via cognitive analysis. Strong feelings about areas of marital conflict may be seen by both partners as getting in the way of effective problem solving. Frequently, affective response is given less legitimacy than cognitive response to a situation. Both spouses have usually had a history of successful achievement using cognitive modes of problem solving in their personal lives, educational preparation, and careers. Their familiarity with verbal, cognitive intellectual skills has resulted typically in the development of certain characteristic psychological defenses. Thus, they frequently resort to intellectualization, rationalization and isolation of affect from thought when faced with anxiety-arousing situations. Such defenses are also those frequently used by many therapists in the face of anxiety; thus, the therapist may have a tendency to label

97

such behaviors as relatively "healthy" and to identify with the couple in this regard.

The process of therapy itself tends to be anxiety arousing at times and, indeed, this is necessary if treatment is to be effective. The dissolving of old, familiar behaviors and defenses leaves the client(s) feeling, literally, defenseless and usually somewhat anxious, until new, more effective coping skills are learned. Given the presence of two or three (if one includes the therapist) verbal, cognitive people, it is easy to see how therapy can quickly become a highly verbal experience. Such verbosity may come to serve primarily defensive purposes, with little if any resultant meaningful behavior change.

It is important that the therapist not merely engage in a verbal repartee with the couple. Although the dual-career couple may prefer solutions to their problems which involve strong cognitive aspects—e.g., working out a time schedule for being together as a couple—it is important that the affective component of their experiences together be addressed regularly. Along the lines of the above example, the most creatively and equitably arranged time schedule will not work for very long if the husband really believes down deep that his wife should pursue her career only if it doesn't result in any inconvenience for him. Behavioral marital therapists have distinguished between "administrative time" and "feeling time" in problem solving by couples (Weiss, 1975). Both aspects of response to a problem situation are necessary, but they may compete for attention and impair efficiency of problem solving. Helping the couple to separate out the administrative task component (the need to arrive at a solution to the problem) from their feelings about the issue or the problem-solving technique itself is a useful therapy procedure. Weiss, Birchler and Vincent (1974) offer excellent prescriptive (stimulus control) guidelines for the effective separation of these two marital problem response aspects.

Because the participants in the couple therapy experience are all likely to be relatively verbal people, it is easy to collude in the direction of seeking premature, verbal solutions to problems with strong affective components. Sometimes cognitive solutions will, indeed, be the fitting and appropriate solutions, with affective components either not needing to be addressed or having already been expressed and taken into account. The therapist must use his or her sensitivity to help the couple deal with both cognitive

98

and affective components, paying attention to the proportion each aspect needs in terms of therapeutic facilitation.

The typical short duration of marital therapy plays into the temptation to arrive at predominantly cognitive solutions. It is the therapist's responsibility to see that this does not happen. The couple cannot always be expected to help in this regard; their defenses and past problem-solving experiences lead them to look usually for intellectual answers to interpersonal problems.

The therapist needs to tune quickly into the affective substrate of the couple's interaction and begin to relate to them on that level. This is necessary to disrupt the couple's "set" and to reorient their responses toward what each is communicating affectively as well as verbally. An example will help to clarify this process:

Case #11. Bruce and Jane were in their early thirties, had been married for six years, and had a son, Paul, age 3. They entered therapy with the complaint that Bruce's extended period of graduate work had kept the family strapped financially and had postponed their having additional children. Jane was a college graduate and had been working for the past five years as an office supervisor. The couple began their second session complaining about the many practical limitations and sacrifices entailed in Bruce's taking so long to finish his dissertation:

BRUCE (B): You know, another thing is, even when I get finished (with the degree) I don't know if I can get a job. You know what the job market is like. Hell, I may have to go to work for the government, in a job that doesn't even require a Ph.D. . . . if I can get that.

JANE (J): What he's saying is that it's gonna be a while before we know where we're going to be.

THERAPIST (T): What does that mean for you?

J: It means I better plan to keep on working.

B: But you want to anyway. Right?

J: Well, not forever. We've talked about having another child at some point.

B: There's plenty of time for that.

T: (to Jane) I hear you trying to tell Bruce that things haven't worked out quite the way you had planned.

J: I didn't plan on his being in school for so long.

T: How do you feel about that?

J: (somewhat defensively) Well, I can understand why it's taken him so long. His major professor certainly hasn't been much help—he's been gone so much. Then he'll rush into town and expect Bruce to have written this and that.

B: Yeah, he does that (half smiling).

T: (to Jane again) I was wondering how you feel about Bruce being in school so long and being unable to plan your life very far ahead.

J: I guess I'm frustrated about how long it's taken. Money has been really tight, since I don't make that much in my job.

T: Do you feel it's been unfair?

J: What?

T: Your having to work for this long to help put Bruce through school.

J: (beginning to show irritation) Yes, sometimes I wake up and think why don't you (Bruce) go off to work and let me stay home and write. Or sleep late.

B: It's not the same; (sarcastically) I'm not writing poetry, you know.

T: I think we're beginning to see how Jane feels rather strongly that things haven't worked out fairly. She feels that she has had to make a lot of sacrifices so that you (Bruce) can keep going to school.

B: But, it's all going to even out once I get a job; (softly) if I get a job.

T: (to Jane) How long will it take to "even things out"?

J: Sometimes it feels like about thirty years (all laugh).

T: I think we need to look more closely at your sense of unfairness. Both of you are saying how you didn't expect things to turn out this way. I'm wondering if there aren't some things you could do for each other to help restore some balance along these lines.

J: Well, Bruce could help by making supper more often. I'm pretty tired when I get home from work.

B: I wouldn't mind doing that. I'm home with Paul in the late afternoon, anyway.

T: That sounds like a good place to start.

This brief excerpt from an early therapy session illustrates some of the difficulties encountered in helping a couple to share their underlying feelings about an agreed-upon problem area. Jane feels empathy for Bruce's situation and this, in some ways, prevents her from expressing the anger she feels toward him. She reveals a certain ambivalence about her own career. On the one hand, she would like Bruce to finish and get a job so she could have the choice of quitting work. On the other hand, she enjoys the independence and autonomy provided by her job and would mainly like more help from Bruce around the house. Any ambivalence that Bruce shows toward his career tends to magnify her own career conflicts. Thus, in one sense, Jane's need for Bruce to finish school and get a job is related to her desire to feel more of a choice about whether to pursue her own career.

The excerpt also illustrates the need for the therapist to be relatively active and somewhat directive, particularly early in therapy, in order to help the partners focus on underlying feelings. It would have been easy to debate with Bruce whether he should be so dependent on his major professor's availability. Although the issue of Bruce's dependency on authority figures (and his resultant anger when they, inevitably, don't come through for him) may be an important topic for later therapy sessions, focusing on this concern could easily have started an intellectual discussion about the role of one's major professor. (There is enough residual feeling in the therapist from his own graduate school experience to be easily "hooked" into such a topic.) Pursuing this would have sidetracked the couple from beginning to deal with the anger resulting from a breakdown in their initial marital contract. (Bruce had been supposed to finish graduate school in five years, they were supposed to have two children three years apart, and Jane was supposed to work half time after the birth of their second child. So much for "the best laid plans. . . .")

In summary, the personality characteristics of individuals who adopt a dual-career life-style have important implications for therapeutic intervention. Use of well developed verbal defenses can lead to an intellectualized approach to problem solving that ignores important underlying feelings. Failure to take this affective substrate into account can eventually undermine the most carefully arrived at solutions to marital problems. The therapist needs to be active and gently directive, particularly early in therapy. It is also important for the therapist in the beginning phases of therapy to offer helpful suggestions and practical advice where possible. For example, the therapist can help the couple devise a time schedule and can share his or her knowledge regarding the way other dual-career couples solve common "overload" problems. The dual-career couple needs to feel some early success by being able to begin resolving their marital dilemmas. This practical early focus can take advantage of their preferred cognitive solutions for interpersonal problems while, simultaneously, beginning to make each partner's underlying feelings more salient. The latter provides a basis for therapy sessions later devoted to the couple's more difficult and/or chronic underlying problems.

·8·

Therapeutic Management of Common Problem Areas

COMMON AREAS of conflict in dual-career marriage (e.g., competition and power issues) were elaborated in Chapter 6. The present chapter will expand on these problem areas, in terms of elaborating specific therapeutic techniques useful in helping couples to deal with such conflicts.

The guiding principle in therapy with dual-career couples is to help the partners achieve or restore a sense of equity in the marital relationship. Although the perception of equity may be important in most intimate relationships (Walster, Walster and Berscheid, 1978), the particular question of felt relationship equity in the facilitation of mutual occupational pursuits usually needs to be addressed with dual-career couples. Since career happiness is typically correlated positively with felt marital happiness for such individuals, perceived relationship inequities in the facilitation of one's career area can lead easily to general marital dissatisfaction. The achievement of a perceived equitable relationship is enhanced if the individuals manifest flexibility and relative freedom from the constraints of gender-role-prescribed behaviors. Weiss (1978), writing from a behavioral standpoint, makes several points in this regard. He states:

> Marriage relationships are governed by *ideologies, stage of their own development, and allocation of resources.* The less a relationship is governed by clearly stated rules (traditional versus egalitarian relationships) the greater the potential for idiosyncratic solutions, that is, far greater trial and error approximations. Relationships based upon beneficial ideologies require considerable accommodation without benefit of seasoned rules to dictate outcomes. (p. 192)

It has been the author's experience that many individuals in dual-career marriages show personality patterns characterized by an above-average degree of rigidity and perseverance. Because of these behavioral characteristics, the therapist is likely to encounter initial resistance in his or her efforts to foster flexibility and openness to new ways of behaving. The therapeutic task is complicated by the fact that the spouses' traits of rigidity and perseverance have been rewarded often by a high degree of educational and occupational achievement. Thus, they are reluctant to modify behaviors that have brought them past success. Given their verbal facility and having a history of being rewarded for verbal behavior, it is easy for them to "tune out" the affective components of their marital experience.

THERAPEUTIC TASKS IN THE EARLY PHASE OF THERAPY

As indicated in Chapter 7, the therapist's task early in treatment is usually to help the couple become aware of underlying feelings related to stated problem areas. This is done by giving feedback, in terms of what the therapist hears the couple "saying" emotionally. The couple's identification with the therapist (in the form of a positive transference) can enhance the effects of the therapist's modeling a comfortable acceptance and expression of feelings. Thus, the early phase of therapy is characterized by an emphasis on helping to balance cognitive and affective communication so that both modes are valued by the couple. Specific behavioral exercises in listening, empathic responding and providing supportive verbal feedback (Gottman *et al.*, 1976; Guerney, 1964) can be especially helpful in this regard. These can be initially demonstrated in the therapy session and then practiced by the couple between sessions. Further discussion and instruction can occur in the following treatment sessions.

As discussed in Chapter 3, the author has found the elaboration of the marital contract (Sager, 1976) especially helpful with dual-career couples. The usual procedure is to instruct the partners to write out (or to develop with the therapist during one or more sessions) their initial marital contract or expectations of one another at the time of marriage. Then the present contract is elaborated, from each partner's perspective. Part of the reason for the current marital difficulties is that each spouse is likely to be operating under a separate individual contract that has probably departed from whatever initial agreement was present. The goal is to focus on the expectations and goal disparities in each partner's separate, individual contract and work with the couple in therapy toward developing a single, agreed-upon contract (Sager, 1976).

Working with a tangible contract is very helpful in the process of restoring perceived equity to the relationship. It helps to concretize vague, subjective feelings that things are "unfair" and show both spouses particular areas that need work in regard to "rebalancing" the marital system along equitable lines. The joint contract can serve as a common frame of reference for the couple's communication about their relationship, thus avoiding the feeling (on both the therapist's and the spouses' part) that they are talking two different "languages." The reader may wish to refer back to the case of Fred and Sarah (Chapter 3) for an example of the use of marital contracts in therapy with a dual-career couple.

The concept of the marital contract, as elaborated by Sager, differs from the issue of behavioral contracts, focused on modification of specific disturbing marital behaviors (see Weiss et al., 1974). In behavioral contracting, the partners usually work out a set of reciprocal behaviors along the lines of "If you do this, then I'll do that." For example, the husband may agree to pick up and hang up his clothes in return for the wife agreeing to make a special meal once a week. Each spouse gives something and gets something he or she desires in return. The therapist helps the couple formulate what is considered to be a fair exchange. Behavioral contracting does deal with the expectations that each spouse has of the other. However, these expectations apply to very focused and specific areas of behavior, and they are stated overtly and available for verbal discussion.

The expectations in the marital contract are typically broader and more general than is the case with behavioral contracting. As discussed in Chapter 3, one important facet of the marital contract has to do with strong covert aspects, which operate out of awareness and yet exert powerful influences on day-to-day behavior. In dealing with the marital contract in therapy, the therapist does not necessarily attempt to have the partners agree that each specific expectation of one spouse will be met by regular, agreed-upon behaviors on the part of the other spouse, as is the case with behavioral contracting.

After establishing rapport and formulating some conceptualization of the sources of marital dysfunction, the therapist's next task in working with dual-career (or other) couples is dealing with resistance to change. Despite the partners' complaints of marital discord, there is often some comfortableness with the way things are. Marital therapists see a fair number of couples who, despite periods of reported unhappiness, have continued their marital relationship. They may state simply, "Our families couldn't take it if we were to get a divorce," or "We're only staying together for the sake of the children." Occasionally, these are not rationalizations, but the genuine reason that the couple has remained married. More often, the pattern of marital bonding is more complex, with the partners bound together through collusion and covert agreement (Stewart et al., 1975). For example, there may be implicit agreement to take care of and protect one another from loneliness. Spouses may boost each other's self-esteem by providing qualities felt to be lacking in one or the other individual.

A major part of the therapist's task in overcoming the couple's initial resistance has to do with pointing out the important, positive things they are getting from the very areas or behaviors that are described as being the source of persistent conflict. A pragmatic way of approaching this is to suggest to the couple, "You wouldn't be continuing to do this (troublesome interaction pattern) unless you were getting something out of it; what do you think that could be?" Thus, the therapist helps the spouses to do a cost-and-benefit analysis of continuing problems. An example will clarify this process.

Case #12. Bill, age 35, and Judy, age 34, have been married for ten years and have two sons, ages 8 and 6. Bill is employed as a sales manager and Judy is a junior high school teacher. The couple entered therapy at Bill's request with the complaint that "Judy is still tied to her mother." On elaboration, it was determined that most of the couple's social life revolved around her parents, who lived in the same city. Judy called her mother practically every day ("just to chat") and Bill had the feeling that mother rather than husband was Judy's main confidante. He resented the time they spent (separately and together) with her family. Bill, however, had not taken active steps to change the situation, preferring instead to snipe at Judy for her continued closeness to her family.

Judy's family was financially comfortable. Her father was an architect. Her mother had not been employed outside the home. Judy had a younger brother, Cliff (age 28), who was not married and was finishing law school. Cliff had majored in business in college and then worked for three years before entering professional school. Judy felt close to both parents, for different reasons. She admired her father's sensitivity ("he's a frustrated artist") and enjoyed their talks about social issues. Judy stated that, following a rebellious period in her teens, she and her mother had again become "friends." Judy noted, "I think it helped once I had kids; that seemed to convince her that maybe I was going to be 'normal' after all." Indeed, both of Judy's parents doted on the two grandchildren and often arranged to take them on special trips, such as going camping, to ball games and to the zoo.

Bill's family lived in a large city approximately two hundred miles away. Bill and Judy would visit, with the children, several times a year, usually around holidays. Bill's father was a semiretired newspaperman. He had had a mild coronary approximately five years before. Following his recovery, on the advice of his physician, he reduced his working hours substantially. Bill's mother ran a small boutique. Bill had an older, married brother who lived in the same city as his parents. His brother and his wife had two children, a son and a daughter. Bill felt a congenial relationship with his parents; however, he felt independent of them, in general, and said that the amount of contact with them "seems just about right." Bill had been heavily involved with athletics during high school and college, and he shared with his father an interest along these lines. He felt more distant from his mother and stated: "Ever since I entered high school, she's been pretty much involved with her store."

Bill and Judy had met during his junior and her sophomore year in college. He had worked as a busboy in the dormitory where she lived. Judy shared his interest in sports and much of their leisure time was spent in playing tennis, going bike riding and swimming. It was a smooth courtship and was the first serious relationship for both, although each had had substantial dating experience. Judy noted: "People said that we looked like we belonged together." During the second year of their relationship, they both worked actively in the campaign of a presidential candidate, having been designated campus co-coordinators. In retrospect, Bill noted: "Doing this seemed to pull us together; it was a nice feeling to feel that we were working jointly for somebody we both believed in."

After Bill graduated, he moved to a medium-sized city, fifty miles from the college town, and took a job with a manufacturing firm. Bill and Judy had agreed that they would "see other people" during that year, partly as a way of "making sure about our relationship." A crisis occurred midway through the year when Bill announced to Judy that he thought he was falling in love with another woman he had been seeing, who worked in data processing at his firm. Judy was concerned, but did not panic. She came to see Bill for a weekend shortly thereafter and they "spent a lot of time talking things out." He decided subsequently that he had put his relationship with Judy "to the test" and that he did want to continue his involvement with her. Both reported in retrospect that this experience helped them to cement their plans to get married, which they did several months after Judy's graduation.

In terms of the couple's presenting problem of Judy's involvement with her mother, Bill stated: "Well, I always knew Judy was close to her folks. I kind of envied her in that way and they seemed to accept me okay." He continued: "I always assumed that once we got married, the ties would lessen. Then, five years ago, I was offered my current position in R—— (where the couple and Judy's parents live). She got all excited and talked about how the kids could be close to Grandma and Grandpa. I was all caught up in the glitter of the job offer and didn't give much thought to how things would be between us and them (her parents)."

During the first few therapy sessions, it seemed clear that neither Judy nor Bill had actively taken steps to set limits on their involvement with her parents. She acknowledged that her relationship with her mother was causing problems for the marriage but felt sharply conflicting loyalties. The growing tension at home was affecting her work and she stated: "Sometimes I feel like I'm losing confidence in myself as a teacher. It's like I have to get home and smooth things out there, that's my first priority. I never really felt that way before. Bill's always given me a lot of support in my job; I mean, he'll cut out articles in the paper that he thinks my classes might be interested in."

The reluctance of the couple to set limits on the relationship with Judy's parents alerted the therapist to the notion that, despite what the contact with her family was "costing" the couple in felt psychological distress, they must be receiving some positive benefits. An excerpt from midway in the third therapy session, during which the "benefits greater than costs" hypothesis is explored, is presented below.

THERAPIST (T): As you've been talking about your feelings about Judy's family, and how much a part of your life they are, I've noticed that neither of you seems to have taken active steps to change matters. Am I right in this?

BILL (B): Well, I've bitched a lot.

JUDY (J): Yeah, to me. But you haven't said anything to them.

B: Neither have you.

J: They're my parents; I don't want to hurt their feelings. They have been pretty good to us.

B: Okay, I agree that's true. But recently I've had a hard time keeping that in mind.

T: (to J) Can you say a little more about what they've done for you?

J: Well, the big thing was they loaned us the money three years ago for a down payment on our house. We hadn't been able to save enough and mortgage money was tight. You had to have a big down payment to get a decent house. We'd probably still be waiting if it was up to us to save up. I don't know where the money goes, but neither Bill nor I are very religious about saving.

T: Did the money come with any strings attached?

J: Oh no. They just said, "Pay us back when you can." (defensively) They could afford it; I mean, Dad's a senior partner in his firm now. They don't have much to spend it for—they go on a few trips each year, but other than that . . .

T: (interrupting) How about psychological strings?

J: I'm not sure what you mean?

T: Did they seem to expect anything in return, other than paying back the money?

B: I think I know what he's getting at. Did taking the money mean we were obligated to them in some other way? Like we were supposed to be grateful children or something.

T: (provocatively) Well, children do stay close to home.

J: And I suppose they feel guilty leaving home, especially if their parents have made it pretty cushy. But I thought I had already left home. That's what all the rebelling, when I was a teenager, was all about. And I went away to college, away from home.

B: You went back a lot of weekends. And most summers.

T: (to J) Can you think of other good things your parents do for you?

J: I suppose you could include all the things they do for Ricky and Danny (their sons). They spoil those little guys rotten and, of course, they eat it up. But it's important for kids to be with grandparents, especially before they get too old to do things with their grandchildren. Don't you think that's part of what's wrong today, with the family, I mean? Kids grow up and move away, and then their kids don't see their grandparents.

B: Let's get off the social issue bit, and get back to us. Hell, Rick and Danny could visit my parents, if the only problem was getting grandparents and grandchildren together. What I'm hearing Dave (the therapist) say is that things we get from your mom and dad have their price. To us. To the marriage. . . . Maybe it's not worth it.

T: Bill, I find myself wondering why you've gone along with Judy's being so involved with her folks. You've bitched to her, but you haven't really put your foot down. Why do you think that is?

B: (pause) Well, if I were to really be honest, I'd have to say that I realize her family can give her some things I can't. Like the money things. She grew up with more money than I did. I think down deep that's what she expects, and I'm afraid I'll let her down. I've just started earning a pretty good salary.

T: Anything else?

B: I guess somebody to talk to. Since I'm on the road about a week out of each month. When I'm not there, and Judy wants to talk to somebody, she just calls her mom. But I think there's been too much of that. It'd be okay during the week but we usually end up going over there at least one night on the weekend.

T: Do you ever feel like she's got more going with Mom than with you?

B: I've thought of that. And then I get pissed.

T: Do you let her see those feelings?

110

B: I'll bitch about going over there.

T: I mean about your fear that some of the closeness you felt with Judy may be slipping away. (silence)

J: Are you really worried about that? Because I talk to Mom?

B: Yes, don't you feel it?

J: Well, not really. I love you both. . . .

B: It's like I'm in some goddamn competition or something.

T: Who's winning?

B: Her mom—her parents.

J: (getting teary) What am I supposed to do? (pause)

T: Let's explore some ways in which the two of you might change things. For instance, I've noticed that you haven't talked about friends—either your own friends or other couples.

B: I don't think we've really made friends here in R——. It gets back to having ready-made friends—her parents, again—when we came.

J: That did make it easy.

T: Can you see any advantage to broadening your social life?

J: You mean so I don't just relate to my parents?

T: Yeah.

In subsequent sessions, the development of other friendships was explored further. Some of the covert resistance in this regard seemed to stem from the fact that Bill's forming a relationship with another woman (in the year after college, while the couple was apart, and before they had a firm commitment to get married) had seriously threatened his and Judy's relationship. This may have led both of them to conclude subconsciously that relationships with parents would be safe from such a threat. This assumption subsequently proved to be a questionable one.

The case illustrates how, despite the couple's protest about the disadvantages of their interlocking with Judy's parents, there were some distinct (financial and emotional) advantages that helped keep the relationship with her parents going. Only recently had the costs begun to outweigh the benefits, at least in Bill's mind, and these feelings had led them to seek marital counseling. Working through the source of their resistance to change, in the sense of their being unable to set firm limits in dealing with Judy's parents, formed much of the initial part of therapy with this couple.

Although dual-career conflicts were not the main focus in the therapy sessions, Judy's tie to her family did affect her career. She had never felt the enhancement of self-esteem that can come with individuation from one's family or origin (Karpel, 1976). Thus, when Judy felt forced to choose between depending emotionally on Bill or on her family, her self-confidence was shaken. These feelings carried over into her job, and she began to lose confidence in her ability as a teacher. In a way, her career functioning was strongly tied to being able to depend on her primary relationships. While generally of comfort, this left her with a certain sense of vulnerability, when these relationships didn't always come through for her in time of need.

Though seemingly more independent of his family, Bill had similar conflicts. He felt dependent on Judy's family providing her with certain things he felt incapable of giving to her. His career performance was not as directly affected as Judy's by these dependent ties. However, continued marital stress seemed likely to eventually take a toll in terms of his occupational endeavors and accomplishments.

As stated earlier in this chapter, the overall goal in marital therapy with dual-career couples is the restoration of a sense of equity in the relationship. It is the author's belief that this goal is important in the treatment of many couples and families, whether or not both partners have careers. The strong emphasis in behaviorally oriented marital therapy on working out fairness contracts and *quid pro quo* behavioral exchange contracts is consistent with the necessity of attending to perceived inequities in any marital relationship (Weiss, Birchler and Vincent, 1974).

Critics of behavioral approaches to the treatment of marital dysfunction have pointed out that such contracting approaches are likely to be limited in usefulness with couples who do not ascribe to an egalitarian ethic in their relationship (Gurman and Knudson, 1978). Since negotiation is a primarily verbal process, both partners need a certain degree of verbal facility in order to negotiate successfully with one another. These skills may need to be practiced with the couple (e.g., using role playing) before negotiation is attempted.

Some of the criticisms of behavioral approaches to marital therapy might also be applicable to the present model of therapy, with its emphasis on perceived relationship equity. The priority given to perceived fairness (of task distribution, career opportunity, etc.) in a relationship is likely to be greater in couples who ascribe to an egalitarian marital ethic. However, given the democratic ethos in this country, and social conditioning along these lines, most individuals have some notion that things in life should be "fair." They are likely to react to perceived unfairness in relationships, whether or not they feel committed to an egalitarian ideology. The frequency of this reaction provides additional support for the notion that equity considerations should be addressed in all couples who come for treatment.

Part of the early phase of therapy is devoted to helping each spouse bring out honest feelings directly, in regard to perceived inequity in the relationship. Sometimes one or both partners do not have the verbal skills needed to express feelings of inequity in a direct and open manner. They may feel guilty about imposing on their spouses such reactions and criticisms. In this case, as with behavioral negotiation, the therapist may need to help the couple practice stating their feelings directly. Role playing of certain situations that are likely to lead to feelings of unfairness can be helpful. A brief example follows.

Case #13. Dick and Janet were in their middle thirties. He was a professor and she was a research associate in a large urban university. They had a son, Todd, age 8. Janet initiated marriage counseling because she felt increasing anger toward Dick. She found herself, over the past several months, wanting to withdraw from him into her job and into her relationship with Todd. These feelings made her anxious and she was unable to state why and how they had originated.

From very early in therapy, it was evident that Dick was more verbally fluent than Janet and able to outtalk her on almost any issue. Sensing futility in the verbal confrontations, Janet, in essence, stopped talking. The therapeutic technique was utilized of having Dick listen during part of the session, while Janet talked. She was asked to focus on events or behaviors on his part that had felt unfair to her. He was then asked to repeat back what he heard Janet saying and what he sensed to be her feelings.

It gradually emerged that Janet felt Dick's numerous out-of-town trips to conventions, for speaking engagements, and as a consultant, left her with an unfair proportion of Todd's care. Her feelings of inequity were compounded by the fact that she had turned down the chance to go on similar professional trips. Thus, she felt she had made the sacrifice of staying home to be with her family, and was angry that Dick had not felt compelled to do the same.

Dick seemed surprised at the intensity of Janet's feelings about his being out of town so much. He asked her: "Why didn't you mention this before?" She replied: "Well, I felt you should have the opportunity to go. You always seem happy when you get back—like you've had your ego boosted, or something." Dick acknowledged that he found the trips professionally stimulating, and sometimes financially rewarding. However, he indicated that he was growing tired of so much traveling. He had the sense also that his colleagues were beginning to question whether he was neglecting his duties at the university, although he had been conscientious in having other professors take over his assignments whenever he was gone.

They were able eventually to negotiate a compromise. He agreed to cut out some trips and she agreed to take advantage of some of her own opportunities for professional travel. Dick said he was "more than willing" to take care of Todd while she was gone, taking away a rationalization Janet had used for staying at home. Later in therapy, Janet indicated that one reason she had not traveled was that she would feel too guilty about not being home to look after her family. She also did not feel the confidence that she could manage things independently, as would be required when traveling alone.

In addition to the negotiation of a more equitable arrangement for *both* partners to take advantage of professional travel opportunities, it was necessary to work through in therapy some of Janet's fears and anxieties about leaving her family and being on her own. As she gained confidence in this regard (partly as a result of attending a convention by herself and "doing okay"), her wish to withdraw from interaction with Dick subsided. He became aware of the need to listen to Janet's feelings and not to rush in and overpower her with words. Communication improved and the couple terminated therapy after ten sessions.

THE MIDDLE PHASE OF THERAPY

Once the initial resistance to changing behavior has begun to decrease and the affective components of the couple's communication have been ascribed a greater legitimacy, therapy moves into a second or middle phase. The middle phase is characterized by the working through of core marital problem areas. Three conflict areas frequently encountered with dual-career couples, as outlined in Chapter 6, will serve as illustrative examples of the process of therapeutic "working through" in the middle phases. These areas are: (a) competition between the spouses, (b) issues of power, and (c) difficulties in arranging a support structure. This list is not meant to be exhaustive of dual-career marital conflicts, but only to be representative. The therapeutic techniques outlined have general applicability to other marital conflict areas. To provide continuity, the case studies presented in Chapter 6 to elaborate the first two conflict areas will also be utilized here. Excerpts from the therapy of each case will be given, in order to illustrate the therapeutic task of working through the problem area.

THERAPEUTIC MANAGEMENT OF COMPETITIVE CONFLICTS

Many dual-career couples feel compelled to suppress natural, and probably inevitable, competitive feelings. Although the traditional socialization of males has generally been supportive and rewarded competitive efforts, most of a man's competitive experience has been largely with other males. It does not feel quite right to acknowledge that one feels competitive with a woman, especially one's wife. Thus, many husbands in dual-career marriages tend to deny that they are competitive with their wives. The outcome of this denial may be perception of a metamessage on the wife's part, along the lines of "women can't handle such competitive feelings."

The socialization history for women in regard to competitiveness is usually different from that for men. Only recently, as witnessed, for example, by the burgeoning interest in women's sports, has competitiveness been generally reinforced and valued as a part of female role development. An indirect result of the need to suppress competitive feelings has led to a "fear of failure" in many women (see review by Hoffman, 1974). More recent findings (Feather and Raphelson, 1974; Monahan, Kuhn and Shaver, 1974) indicate that fear of failure (or its antithesis, expectation of success) can occur in both men and women. Thus, fear of failure is not disproportionately distributed by gender, when males and females are both raised in an environment where significant others foster the anticipation of success (and reinforce strivings for competitive achievement).

Given the developmental conflicts surrounding competitive feelings between men and women, it is not surprising that such feelings tend to be suppressed or denied. Therefore, the therapist is confronted with the task of helping dual-career couples to overcome their resistance about acknowledging competitive feelings and the reaction to such feelings, particularly anger, bitterness and disappointment. Accompanying such resentment is often a sense of perceived inequity. Dual-career spouses inevitably compare one another's careers and the result can be a painful, felt sense of unfairness, which ultimately becomes difficult to rationalize.

The by-products of competitive feelings appear in many ways, some of which may have been present for a long time, but not expressed directly. Thus, a wife may resent a move of many years ago, to which she acquiesced in order that her husband could take advantage of a better job offer. The fact that she was traditionally expected to make such a sacrifice of her own career wishes can work against her bringing out and facing feelings of long-standing resentment. Yet the effects of such feelings are likely to be shown in various indirect ways within the marital interaction, e.g., in affectional withdrawal. The therapist's task is to help bring such feelings out in the open, where they can be dealt with directly by the spouses. Then the process can begin of restoring a sense of equity to the relationship.

Many couples are understandably reticent to unearth old grievances. The fear is that once the anger surrounding a specific situation is expressed, the floodgates will be opened and a torrent of pent-up hostility will come forth. The therapist can help to reassure the couple in this regard, while at the same time creating a supportive atmosphere in which each spouse can begin to bring out suppressed feelings. People who have learned effective ways of suppressing anger (in the sense that such defensive behaviors have reduced anxiety) do not usually forego these all at once. Typically, a little anger is let out and, if this is accepted and one feels "safe," more resentment can then be expressed gradually. The therapist can serve as a catalyst in this process, creating a comfortable climate for the expression of feelings and helping the couple to acquire listening and empathic skills that will permit each spouse truly to "hear" what the other is saying.

The goal in uncovering and expressing competitive feelings and their residual anger is not primarily that of catharsis. Indeed, there is little evidence that catharsis, *per se,* is therapeutic (Marshall, 1972). There is usually not a great sense of relief when long-standing resentment is brought out. The most common feeling may be one of mild apprehension, a common initial response to having mastered a new skill, about which one formerly felt some conflict. The therapeutic value of bringing such feelings "out in the open" lies in the fact that it (a) opens up more available channels of direct communication for the couple, and (b) redefines some basic operating ground rules about the degree of direct feeling expression, i.e., it redefines the relationship itself. By knowing directly how one's spouse feels about a situation, one does not have to resort to guessing why he or she is "mad." Many marital therapists feel that a lot of obfuscating, time and relationship consuming, interpersonal games can be avoided by the spouses being able to communicate directly and openly (Miller, Nunnally and Wackman, 1975). This is one reason why so much of the therapist's efforts are directed toward the goal of improving communication in both the cognitive and affective modes.

Case #9 (continued). In order to illustrate some of the above therapeutic tasks, Case #9 (Chapter 6) is further examined, with excerpts presented from that part of therapy which dealt with the working through of competitive feelings. It will be recalled that Jan, age 33, and Eric, age 34, had been married for ten years and had two children, Tommy, age 8, and Beth, age 6. Eric had achieved rapid success as a university professor and then, at the peak of his career, left academia to work for the government, necessitating a move to a different city. Jan had increasingly resented Eric's temporal and emotional absence from the family, especially since she had, to a certain extent, "sacrificed" her own career. Jan had resumed her graduate studies and was in the process of writing her dissertation at the time the family left for Eric's new job.

The early therapy sessions were focused on exploring the couple's family backgrounds and the pressures that had been placed on each spouse by their respective families. Eric indicated that it had always been expected that he would do well and he had not essentially rebelled against such expectations. Jan said that her mother's career abandonment, in order to have children, was supported by her father. This had, in some ways, made it seem natural for Jan to interrupt her own career plans when Tommy was born. She felt, however, that her mother would have a greater current sense of satisfaction with her life had she resumed her career. Jan noted, "She keeps talking about it (updating her nursing certification) but I don't think she's going to do it. My dad doesn't say anything, one way or the other, except that I know he wouldn't want her working as his nurse."

It seemed clear from the family histories that Eric's family was more directly encouraging of his achievement than was Jan's family. They were careful to insure that Eric had good teachers in elementary and high school, and they sent him to a special "science camp" for two summers. Jan could sense her resentment early in their relationship over the fact that Eric's parents facilitated his education and, indirectly, his professional accomplishment. She had not received nearly as much support and encouragement from her family in terms of her own educational and occupational aspirations. However, she held these feelings in check because "to express this would be like criticizing my parents. And that wouldn't really be fair; they did a lot for me, and I know they've wanted me to be happy."

It can be seen how Jan's developmental experiences in some ways left her without a strong sense of external support for any career aspirations. Having that support might have enabled her to assert her own later preferences in this regard. As it was, she did not protest the ostensibly mutually-arrived-at decision to interrupt her own career preparation in order to have children. It was only later, when she felt unfairly treated by Eric's withdrawal from family responsibilities, that her stored-up anger began to lead to emotional alienation from the marital relationship.

The therapist approached the task of working on the couple's competitive feelings from the standpoint that bringing these out in the open would be facilitative for the relationship. The general goal was to help the spouses see more clearly the source of Jan's feelings of inequity and to lay the groundwork for ultimately restoring a sense of perceived fairness in the marriage. Part of this process involved helping Eric to talk about the sense of loss he had felt over his lack of involvement with Tommy and Beth, which had occurred as a by-product of his rush to get ahead academically.

The initial efforts at dealing with competitive feelings began in the fifth therapy session. Jan had started to talk about her feelings of having interrupted her graduate studies just prior to Tommy's birth.

JAN (J): I remember we were both excited about the baby. It was getting a little cumbersome to get around and the semester was ending. It seemed a good time to quit, and that's the way we had planned it.

THERAPIST (T): Did you have any doubts about whether you were doing the right thing?

J: Not then—at least I don't remember any. (to Eric) Do you think I did?

ERIC (E): I remember you thought you might be letting Professor J—— down. He wanted you to continue, but maybe he just wanted you to help him out with his own research.

J: He had been pretty good to me. I didn't feel like I was being exploited.

T: (sensing the couple getting away from the topic at hand) Jan, how do you feel now about having stopped then?

J: Well, with all the great advantage of hindsight, I can see it was a mistake. You know, I really thought that it was okay for Eric to go ahead, almost like he could do well for both of us.

T: I think that's a common feeling, but it can sometimes involve giving up one's identity to live kind of vicariously through someone else. Sooner or later, you have to face up to the issue of who *you* are.

J: Yeah.

E: (defensively) I'm not sure what all that means for me. I obviously couldn't have stayed home and had the baby.

J: It would have helped if you had stayed home, at least some more of the time, *after* I had Tommy and after Beth.

E: You know it was important to both of us for me to get tenure.

J: Yes, but it was important for me to have some help at home. It's not just that, I could have managed. But I wanted you there just for companionship, and to share more of Tommy's and Beth's growing up.

E: (resignedly) I know. I feel badly about that now. (Long pause. Jan's pain over the loss of companionship and Eric's pain over his lack of involvement with the children seem evident to both

119

partners. However, the therapist senses they are both currently at a loss as to how to undo this pain and decides to leave the area for exploration in future therapy sessions.)

T: (to Jan) I have some sense that you're still expecting Eric to come through for you with certain things that you may ultimately have to provide for yourself.

J: Like what?

T: A better sense of who you are and what you want. In some ways this seems to have been lost when you abandoned your own career plans.

E: (interrupting) Jan's been talking about going back to school.

T: (to Eric) How would you feel about that?

E: It would be all right with me. We'd have to hire someone to look after the kids.

J: (sarcastically, to the therapist) You see what he's really concerned about. It's okay just as long as it doesn't disrupt his work.

T: Would his feelings about that serve to keep you from doing it—from going back to school?

J: A couple of years ago it would have. But I've got to do something. I'm resenting Eric's not being home more and more and I'm getting bitchier with the kids—like I'm taking it out on them.

T: Have you taken it out on Eric?

E: She isn't very friendly when I do get home. I thought it was just the strain of being with the kids.

T: I hear Jan saying that it's more than that, that the feelings are deeper.

E: (to the therapist) Do you think she's sorry she quit grad school?

T: (to Eric) Why don't you ask *her*?

E: (to Jan) Are you (smiles nervously)?

J: Yes, but there was a good reason. But I'm even sorrier that it didn't stop with that. I mean, I kept having to take over at home while you went on with your career. (with rising anger) How do you think that's made me feel?

E: I . . . I don't know.

J: Like you're getting farther ahead while I'm falling back. It isn't a very good feeling.

E: What do you want me to do about it?

J: How about helping me out for a change?

E: How?

J: Would you really support my going back to school? I'm a little scared, you know—I'd have to go back and pick up some things—like taxonomic classification. God, I've forgotten so much of that.

E: Maybe I could help out a little. I remember feeling proud of you when we were in grad school. I didn't feel like I wanted to hold you back—it just happened.

T: (to Eric) It seems to have left Jan feeling very resentful of you. And *you* must resent her coldness and distance.

E: I do, because I don't feel I've truly done anything to deserve that.

T: Do you have any better idea now—about where her feelings are coming from?

E: Yes, but I'm not really sure what I can do about it. Other than support her going back to school.

T: Why don't you two talk about what you would really like, and need, from each other if Jan were to go back to grad school. You might even try drawing up a "contract"—not the Mafia kind (laughter)—that would spell out each of your expectations from the other. Bring in what you have next time and, if you'd like, I'll be glad to go over it with you and help with any rough spots.

It will be noted that, in this initial introit into the area of the couple's competitive feelings, the label "competition" was not used. Given the connotations of the word and the defensiveness it can arouse, it is better often to encourage the expression of accompanying feelings, particularly anger, first. There is usually plenty of time to interpret the generic source of the specific resentments as related to a sense of competition between the spouses. At that later time, the therapist can then help the couple to see that it is perhaps natural for two achievement-oriented people to feel, at times, competitive with one another. In fact, the restoration of equity can often be served by a "fair" acceptance of these needs in both partners. Ultimately, mutual competitiveness may become synergistic, with each partner helping to spur the other toward more productive and more satisfying accomplishment.

121

THERAPEUTIC MANAGEMENT OF POWER ISSUES

Chapter 6 elaborated the hypothesis that power conflicts occur in dual-career marriage partly from the fact that both partners have "resource power." By virtue of educational and occupational attainments, they each bring to the relationship qualities which are seen in other, more traditional relationships as scarce and desirable, e.g., the capability of financially supporting oneself independent of one's spouse. This means that they have potentially greater freedom to leave the relationship. If they remain together, it is because they choose to, rather than "have to." Thus, each partner in a dual-career marriage has a substantial amount of effective power, and this can be used productively or destructively in the relationship.

If one partner decides to use his or her power overtly against the other, the usual response is for the partner on the receiving end to use an indirect power maneuver to even the score, thus restoring a tentative balance to the relationship and avoiding a knock-down, drag-out battle. For example, if the husband receives a better job offer in a different geographical location and decides to take it (without careful consideration of his spouse's opportunities), the wife has several choices. She may state her opposition directly, feeling that her position is justified based on her felt rightful share of personal influence over the major decisions made by the couple. If her spouse still shows a reluctance to consider her feelings, even when she has expressed them forthrightly, an ultimatum may be the result. In this case, she may use her power overtly and declare, "If you go, I'm staying here, and that's it for the marriage." At the other extreme, if she feels unable to assert her feelings directly, she may agree to go along and subsequently make her husband's life miserable through bitchiness, criticism aimed at undermining his success, and/or ultimate self-denigration via prolonged, halfhearted efforts to find a job for herself. Given an unsatisfactory resolution of the issue, the emotional component of the relationship can soon begin to break down. It is at this point that the couple may seek marital therapy.

As indicated for the previously discussed conflicts around competition (which are certainly not antithetical to power issues), the therapist's task is to help bring the underlying power struggle "out in the open." Then each partner's feelings can be evaluated as to their legitimacy and impact on the relationship. It would, for example, generally be considered "illegitimate" for a husband to undermine his wife's efforts at career achievement purely because of his own success neurosis, which may relate to his inability to leave his family of origin and take on adult roles (Freud, 1916).

Once the feelings of both partners which resulted in the power struggle have been expressed directly and openly, the therapeutic task is then one of restoring a sense of equity to the relationship. The concept of equity acknowledges that, while the two spouses have somewhat different needs, the relationship should offer each partner a fair chance of having his or her needs met. In elaborating this position, as it applies to the need for sharing control and determination in a marital relationship, the author has previously stated: "We operate from the hypothesis that a sharing of overt and socially recognized power leads to enhanced self-esteem and promotes personal growth for both individuals" (Rice and Rice, 1977, pp. 5–6). Although this comfortable sharing of power in a relationship may represent the ideal endpoint, there are many reality constraints that work against this position. Because of the association between socially recognized power and one's felt status and self-esteem, it is perhaps natural to wish to maintain the degree of power one has in a relationship. From a pragmatic standpoint, several conditions need to be present before one is willing to let go and share some of the influence or determination he or she feels in a relationship. Prominent among these conditions is a sense of respect for the basic competence of the person who seeks to share power with the individual ascribed as having it. Equally important is a sense of trust. Each partner needs to feel that the other will not use power destructively. For example, a husband may not be willing to turn over the management of the couple's finances (though he might prefer to do so) if he is convinced his wife is a spendthrift. Or a wife may hesitate to let her husband participate actively in the care of a small child if she is afraid he might physically (even unintentionally) harm the child. In the latter case, the lack of trust may relate to an isolated instance of physical abuse suffered during an angry confrontation earlier in the marriage.

Before the partners can work on comfortably sharing power, they must usually deal with building or restoring basic relationship ingredients, such as trust and respect. This is often the marital therapist's general goal in helping a couple. For dual-career spouses, the gaining of a sense of respect for the basic competence of both individuals, particularly in non-sex-role stereotyped areas, is perhaps easier than for traditional couples. This respect is based on both partners in a dual-career marriage having access to socially recognized resource power and influence in the relationship via their educational and occupational attainments, as discussed previously. Respect for the intellectual competence of each individual was often an important part of the initial attraction of the partners to one another. In this important area, at least, there is usually a history of felt respect for one another. Through opening up communication, the therapist can use this prior experience to help the couple restore basic respect to the relationship.

Helping dual-career spouses to regain a sense of trust is often a more difficult task. This is partly because feelings of trust may not have a tangible anchor point to refer back to, as do feelings of respect. The latter can be related specifically to actual educational and occupational attainments. Of the two qualities, trust appears to be somewhat more fragile than respect for dual-career couples. Trust may be more subject to day-to-day variation and the nuances of a single incident, e.g., betraying a confidence to another person. Of course, enough instances of loss of trust will eventually summate in a loss of respect.

A key element in feeling trust for one's spouse has to do with the notion of "good will." In any relationship, close moments together and shared positive experiences build up a reservoir of good feelings. During stressful and conflictual periods, remembering the good times together is helpful for restoring perspective on the relationship and decreasing felt ambivalence. With sustained conflict, the sense of good will is usually depleted. A significant number of couples who come to marital therapy appear to be in the state where remembering or anticipating positive experiences together is no longer able to compensate for felt current problems. They lack a sense of basic trust in one another.

Helping the couple to reestablish trust is often a slow and delicate process for the therapist. Previously having been hurt psychologically by one's spouse leads to a reluctance to risk trusting again. A vicious circle results, since only by risking can one test out whether the spouse is trustworthy. Once direct channels of communication are opened, the therapist can gently encourage both partners to trust one another with sensitive feelings. If the spouse is accepting of sensitive communication and is nonretaliatory, a modicum of trust is engendered. Repeated experiences along these lines strengthen a sense of trust.

Once the couple has been helped therapeutically to restore the basic qualities of respect and trust to their relationship, they are more easily able to share power and control. Each trusts that the other will not abuse the relationship control he or she possesses, partly out of respect for the feelings of the spouse. To summarize, with dual-career couples: "The general therapeutic goal is working toward an . . . (equitable) sharing of overt power, with social, economic, and political considerations and intrapsychic forces given comparable consideration" (Rice and Rice, 1977, p. 3).

Case #10 (continued). An example of the therapeutic process utilized in restoring trust and respect and for resolving power issues can be illustrated for the case of Don and Sally, presented in Chapter 6. It will be recalled that the spouses were in the same professional field and had been married for two years. They were finishing a second year of postdoctoral training and had begun to look for jobs. Sally, perceived as more "intellectually competent" by both partners, had obtained an attractive job offer. Don, labeled the more "socially competent," did not have a position, due in part to his own inertia, and began, for the first time in the marriage, silently to feel resentment toward Sally. He sought individual therapy to deal with these troubling feelings and the therapist suggested that Sally join the sessions.

In the tenth session, Don has been talking about his ambivalence in regard to his mother's expectations that he would "do well."

DON (D): Sometimes I've wondered if I'm supposed to make up for something that is missing in her (his mother's) life. She's an artist, a commercial artist really, but I don't think it is challenging enough for her. She can only go so far in her job. I think that's frustrating to her.

THERAPIST (T): How does she feel about your father's success?
D: It's hard to tell. She thinks some of his colleagues are a pretty stuffy bunch. (pause)
T: Do you think she's jealous?

125

D: Of his freedom, yes. I mean, being a professor he doesn't have to punch a time clock. He can come home in the afternoon.

T: (one more try) How about feeling jealous of his success?

D: I'm not sure. Do you mean is she trying to live vicariously through his success?

T: Or through yours.

D: Well, I can see that. I've felt her pressure there, and you know that I've thought "damned if I'll give her what she wants." (pause)

T: (to Sally) Does all this have any meaning for you?

SALLY (S): Well, I know some about Don's battle with his mother. But she's been good to me and I don't feel like I'm a part of that (struggle).

T: I was thinking more along the lines of how Don handles your expectations of him, particularly in regard to next year and getting a job. (Sally has her job offer at this point.)

D: I'm not sure what she expects.

S: Well, I've tried not to say anything that would upset him. He's been looking around ("finally" was implied, but not said) . . . and he did interview at A——.

T: Could you state your expectation clearly and directly to Don—about next year? I feel you've been protecting him from some of your feelings and I'm not sure he needs that.

S: (to Don) Well, it would be easier on both of us if you got a good job.

D: You sound like my mother.

S: Well, I'm not. (pause)

T: (rhetorically, to Sally) Do you think he often tends to get the two of you mixed up?

D: (to therapist) Oh, you're not gonna give me any of that Freudian bullshit . . . that Sally is really my mother?

T: (feeling Don's criticism arousing some of his own ambivalence regarding orthodox Freudian thinking) Well, not exactly. What I am saying is that the pattern of your never having *directly* confronted your mother's expectations, or those of certain important other people, may have carried over into the marriage. The withdrawal you each sense from the other may parallel somewhat this earlier distantiation in your life.

S: (partly colluding with the therapist) I think what Dave (the therapist) is saying makes some sense. I have been holding back, because I couldn't understand why you weren't talking to me lately. I've felt like I couldn't feel good about the offer at C——, because you didn't have a job yet and you'd resent mine.

D: It's hard to say about that. I have mixed feelings. I'm happy for you—I guess—but I'm scared I won't get anything good. . . . I don't know what that will do to us. Things have been pretty smooth up to now.

S: Maybe that's because we've both been holding back.

T: Not just the negative feelings, but maybe positive ones, too— like affection.

S: I can see that. But I'm still not real clear what all this has to do with Don's mother.

T: I think you've become unsuspectingly involved in a struggle that's been going on inside him for some time.

D: How can we get her out?

T: There's this Greek play, see. . . . (laughter) Seriously, I think it would help to start talking directly about what you feel would be fair next year. How could you work it out so that one of you doesn't feel at a great disadvantage? It probably sounds like a broken record by now, but you can start the process going by stating directly and clearly what each of your expectations is for the other—for next year, and beyond. You might try writing these down, and let me see next time what you come up with.

In subsequent sessions, the therapist worked with the couple toward arriving at a single, mutual contract (Sager, 1976) which could help restore a sense of equity to the relationship and sustain them into the next year. Don gained a greater appreciation of how the power struggle with his mother had carried over into his relationship with Sally. The task was made easier when Don got his job offer and therapy ended shortly thereafter. The couple was seen for a total of fifteen sessions.

THERAPEUTIC INTERVENTION REGARDING THE MARITAL SUPPORT SYSTEM

In helping the couple toward an equitable arrangement re-garding the marital support structure, the therapist's task is often one of providing practical advice and information. This does not imply that there are likely to be no underlying psychological conflicts in this area. Indeed, for many husbands, the question of sharing in domestic and child-care activities strikes at the heart of gender identity conflict and insecurity. The wife's neurotic guilt over simultaneously working and being a mother can be easily aroused by her spouse, colleagues, friends and neighbors. If all the above fail, the media can also be counted on to stir up such guilt feelings periodically. These underlying conflicts are usually addressed in therapy when dealing with more general issues, such as whether the wife will continue to pursue her career after the birth of a child.

Focusing on how the support structure is arranged is, in part, a pragmatic task, and how successfully the couple handles this area early in therapy can provide useful assessment information about their willingness to cooperate toward solving other problems that do not have so obvious an etiology or solution. Help in dealing with the support structure can also give the couple some feeling of mild success early in therapy, when their ambivalence about needing to seek professional help for their marriage and the wish to terminate therapy prematurely may be the greatest.

The author maintains that dual-career couples cannot exist without a "schedule," though it is surprising how many of them try to do so, feeling that things will work out "in good faith." They rarely do, at least not for long, because unanticipated events (e.g., when a child gets sick and one spouse has to stay home) strain the best intentions and test the good will built up between the partners.

As noted earlier (Chapter 5), many couples resent the regimentation implied by having a schedule for assignment of domestic and child-care activities, feeling that their home life should be free from the type of organization and time demands which punctuate their working days. The therapist can work around this resistance by indicating to the couple that "most people find after a while they really don't need to keep referring back to the schedule. Each person knows what needs to be done and, most of the time, does it with a sense of cooperation and for mutual benefit. Unexpected or unusual events do have to be negotiated and arranged, but having the schedule already in existence helps to fit these in because each person knows better where he or she can give or take."

Ideally, the couple works out their own schedule (and negotiates what part of the workload will be turned over to outside help) following some general suggestions and guidelines from the therapist. One helpful "rule" in this regard is that, overall, each partner should feel that the type of task and amount of work are distributed fairly. If the partners are unsuccessful in negotiating on their own, either because communication has broken down or because underlying issues and conflicts keep getting in the way, then helping the couple improve their communication skills is often the therapist's first task. The resultant direct stating of each partner's feelings may, in addition, help provide insight into the source of underlying conflicts (e.g., questions about appropriate masculine and feminine role behaviors). Any resistance to negotiation should be brought out and labeled as such, with the therapist noting: "We may want to delve into the sources of this more, later on." Once communication is improved, the therapist may actually construct a schedule with the couple, acting alternately as negotiator, mediator and/or referee. An example from the case of Ron and Claire (presented in Chapter 5) will clarify this procedure.

Case #6 (continued). Ron and Claire were in their early forties and had a son, age 14, and a daughter, age 12. Though generally occupationally successful they had felt distant from one another for some time and had turned to the children for much of their emotional gratification. Although the couple began therapy "for themselves," when their son began to act out inappropriately, the whole family was eventually seen in therapy. During the early "couple" sessions, Ron voiced the feeling that their system for dividing up domestic and child-care task responsibilities had started to break down, along with an increased inability to communicate with one another. The therapist sensed that working on restoring a more equitable balance in task distribution might be a useful initial therapeutic task, the success of which could sustain later working on more pervasive difficulties in the relationship.

Ron complained specifically that Claire would often get home late and he would be forced to start supper for the family (previously, they had agreed that this was to be "her task"). She countered his complaint with the observation that the house was getting more cluttered and disorganized, and that things were not being put away in the family and living rooms ("his task"). She added, "He never throws anything away; you know, we must have *Time* all the way back to 1950 in the basement."

The therapist sensed that a renegotiation of the couple's domestic and child-care schedule was called for and both spouses agreed readily with this idea. It was suggested that they try to work out a revised schedule during the following week and to bring in the results of their efforts. Some general guidelines were suggested by the therapist. The fact that they had set up a previous schedule suggested that they were likely to be capable of doing this task on their own. The following week they returned with a schedule, and the session began around this topic.

THERAPIST (T): Well, how did it go?

CLAIRE (C): We actually came up with two schedules, Ron's and mine.

T: I take it there's some difference (laughter). Have you made any effort to put them together?

RON (R): A little. Here's the beginnings of a joint schedule (hands same to T). I think we need your help.

T: This looks like a good start. Does it differ much from the old schedule?

R: Not really, the schedule isn't the problem. We're good at that—it's sticking to it that's the problem.

T: What seems to go wrong?

C: He (Ron) may fail to do something one day, and I find myself getting stirred up inside because I can't trust that he's going to do it.

R: Same thing happens to me.

T: You mean not being able to trust that Claire will do her things?

R: Yeah.

T: (making a deliberate decision not to work on the more difficult issue of trust, at this point in therapy) That sounds like a somewhat different issue, and maybe we can get into that later. I also notice on here that you haven't scheduled any time for yourselves, just to be together with one another. You'll remember that I suggested you might want to work that in.

C: I think it's a good idea, but after we get the kids down, there isn't much time left.

One reason for this is that each spouse spent a great deal of time putting "his" or "her" child to bed, since this was a time and

130

occasion for getting emotional gratification and closeness from another person, partly as a compensation for what each spouse was missing from the other.

T: (to Ron) How do you feel about it?

R: About what?

T: Time for you and Claire.

R: I'm willing to give it a try, if we can agree on a time.

T: A lot of couples find that in the evening, after the kids have gone to bed, is probably a good time. We're only talking about a half hour or so. Shall we put that into the schedule and give it a try?

C: Okay with me. (Ron nods affirmatively)

T: How about the other parts of the schedule, where you haven't been able to agree, can we work on those? Or do you sense something else—some other feelings—perhaps the problems with trust you talked about earlier, getting in the way when you try to work that out?

R: It's not going to work if Claire keeps coming home late—at least as long as she's supposed to get supper ready.

T: (to Ron) Could you perhaps take over that job in exchange for something else?

C: I'd be willing to straighten the house in the morning. Ron's supposed to do that, but he hasn't been doing it—at least I don't think he has—there's some disagreement about whose standards are to be followed. Anyway, I don't leave for work as early as he does, and I could do it. If he'd start supper in the evening.

R: Fine with me. I'm usually home then anyway, with the kids.

T: You might want to talk about the "standards" issue. Some couples work out an agreement that whoever does that task, his or her standards apply, and the other person agrees to live with that. If the other one has more stringent standards, maybe he or she would then want to take over that particular task in exchange for something else. Now, how about the other areas where you disagree?

The couple's willingness to negotiate and exchange in the brief excerpt presented above was regarded by the therapist as a hopeful sign. Indeed, the couple was able to arrive at a workable schedule and facilitative communication in that area was restored.

131

They had less success in arranging a consistent time to be together. This seemed to be related to their underlying conflicts around intimacy. Thus, their experience of difficulty with that part of the schedule provided further grist for the therapeutic mill. This was more extensively dealt with in subsequent sessions.

In summary, the present chapter has focused on the therapeutic treatment of three common problem areas in dual-career marriage: competition, issues of power and difficulties with the support structure. The general goals have been facilitation of direct communication, bringing out underlying conflictual feelings, and restoration of trust, respect and a perception of equity to the relationship. Brief excerpts from therapy sessions with several different dual-career couples were presented. These brief glimpses at the therapeutic process do not truly provide a sense of the overall experience of treating such couples. For this reason, an extended case study, focused on the treatment of one dual-career couple, is presented in the Appendix. The common problem areas dealt with in this chapter were all present, to some extent, in the treatment experience with the couple in the extended case study. The next chapter deals with additional therapeutic matters, specifically, the use of co-therapists and the issue of an "individual" versus "couple" problem focus.

·9·

Special Treatment Techniques

THIS CHAPTER will focus on several additional therapeutic issues and strategies to be considered in the treatment of dual-career couples. The author has emphasized primarily the treatment of such individuals within a conjoint marital therapy format, i.e., both spouses and one therapist. Variations of this format can include either adding a co-therapist or seeing several couples in group therapy.

Hopkins and White (1978) suggest group treatment as helpful for dual-career couples. They propose including couples at different stages of the marital life cycle who might share their experiences in facing common dual-career dilemmas. This might be of benefit to younger couples in particular. Other than the Hopkins and White proposal, however, little has been written about group therapy for dual-career couples. The literature on co-therapy is more extensive, although it has not been written specifically for the treatment of dual-career marriage.

UTILIZING CO-THERAPISTS

The co-therapy format has some advantages for treating dual-career couples. Chief among these is the role model provided by the interaction of the two professional co-therapists, particularly if a male and female co-therapist team is utilized. However, there is no empirical support for the notion that two therapists uniformly produce more effective treatment outcomes than a single therapist (Gurman and Kniskern, 1978). Whether co-therapists are more effective when treating dual-career couples—e.g., because of the specific role models provided—has not been investigated.

The use of professional spouse co-therapists might seem a "natural" format. In this case, therapists who themselves form a dual-career couple treat a patient couple with a similar marital life-style. The author has used this treatment format and found it helpful, particularly for the small number of couples who express a preference for working with therapists who are married to each other. The advantages and disadvantages of this treatment format are discussed in the study by Rice, Razin and Gurman (1976). Experienced and inexperienced spouse and nonspouse professional co-therapists answered a questionnaire regarding their "style" of in-therapy behavior. The questions focused on preferred in-therapy activity level, attitudes toward openness and the sharing of one's own feelings with clients, the therapists's preferred degree of control in the therapy situation, etc. The results indicated that experienced *spouse* co-therapists were significantly more alike in independently reported in-therapy behavior style than co-therapists in the other experimental groups. It was suggested that co-therapists married to each other may thus present a strongly "united front" to their clients. While this may increase the degree of impact of their interventions, it could possibly take away a degree of freedom for client(s) to disagree with the therapists' interpretations and suggestions. The Rice, Razin and Gurman (1976) study did not assess treatment outcome. Thus, the issue of the general effectiveness of spouse co-therapists has not been substantively tested from an empirical standpoint.

The author has found that a male and female co-therapist dyad seem particularly likely to foster a parental transference. This is not surprising when one realizes that the experience of relating to male and female authority figures in some ways re-creates for the couple the situation each may have experienced with his or her own parents. The inherently regressive nature of psychotherapy may also foster this type of transference, in that the clients are in an essentially dependent, help-seeking position. Perceiving the co-therapists as parents can, however, have a potentially positive benefit. One or both partners may be seeking a "reparenting" that makes up for certain felt deficiencies in their upbringing and results in increased self-esteem. An illustration of this process can be found in Case #7, presented in Chapter 5, which involved a couple seen by male and female co-therapists.

Case #7 (continued). Frank and Ellen were in their late twenties and were the parents of three small children. They initially entered therapy following Ellen's feelings of increasing desperation with her life situation and her threat of suicide. She had quit college and felt tied down with three closely spaced children. Feeling the need to expand her life beyond home and family, Ellen had gone to work as a hospital aide on a part-time basis. However, she was frustrated with the low pay and felt unchallenged by the nature of her work. She realized that getting a more fulfilling job would likely require that she go back to college and finish getting her degree. The initial period of therapy terminated after Ellen made the decision to go back to college; however, the sessions resumed approximately eight months later and continued off and on for two and one half years.

Over the course of therapy, it became clear that each had fought a long-standing battle with self-esteem. Ellen's father had given her the impression that she couldn't do anything quite good enough to please him. She had largely suppressed her anger over her father's unrealistic expectations and had worked hard to achieve educationally in order to win his favor. Her mother was less critical of Ellen's behavior but did not truly provide an equal measure of support for her daughter, that might have served as a counterweight to the expectations of her father.

Frank's father was a kind man but remained somewhat distant from his son, appearing rather self-contained. Frank had "picked up" this quality and tended to hold his feelings inside, which caused Ellen much frustration. She felt that his withholding of feelings had noticeably impaired their communication, although as a power maneuver, his behavior served as an effective neutralizer of Ellen's ready expressiveness. Frank also had the sense that his father held high expectations for him, although he was not at all sure what these expectations were. This contributed to his feelings of low self-confidence. His mother was much like Ellen's, supportive, but not a strong counterforce to the impact of his father's conditional acceptance.

It became clear to the co-therapists (who were married, but not to each other) that each of the partners was, in part, seeking a "good parent." Both spouses tended to subtly overvalue the male co-therapist—e.g., addressing questions primarily to him—and this was consistent with the more overtly powerful role that each

135

spouse had ascribed to the father in the families of origin. This behavior was also viewed as a subtle attempt to split the co-therapists and render their impact on the marital system less effective. The co-therapists generally resisted the couple's efforts along these lines, attempting to acknowledge openly in the sessions the value of each therapist's respective contributions for the couple and for one another. Indeed, much of the change in the marriage over the course of therapy seemed the result of Ellen introjecting positive valuing from the female co-therapist, with resultant enhanced feelings of self-esteem. This was acknowledged by Ellen in the later therapy sessions.

An excerpt from the therapy with this couple, which deals with the parental transference to the co-therapists, is presented below. The couple had been seen for approximately one year at this point (the excerpt is from near the end of the twentieth session). Ellen has been describing some problems with school during much of the therapy session. At one point she notes that she feels stronger now, and could survive if the couple were to get a divorce.

FEMALE CO-THERAPIST (FT): (to Ellen) We've really focused on you this time. How do you feel about that?

ELLEN (E): Well, as I told Frank when he called me at noon and asked, "What are you doing?", I said, "Thinking of all the things we're going to talk about today." And he said, "Why are you doing that?" And I said, "Cause I think I'm going to go in there and feel like a bad little girl." Like I've done naughty things—somehow that's the way I always feel when I walk in here, but that's not the way I feel when I leave.

MALE CO-THERAPIST (MT): (to FT) What do you think that says about us?

FT: (laughing) I'm not sure.

MT: We're a couple of parents, huh? You got to report in.

FT: We must be good parents though, through the sessions, we . . .

E: (interrupting) Look, I walk in here feeling guilty about the way that I do things, or look, or feel, or whatever, and you sort of say, "Well, that's okay." I mean, well, I guess that's what a parent should do to a child.

At this point, Ellen begins to feel defensive about having taken up so much of the hour for herself. This is exacerbated by Frank's quietness, although he is alert and listening. His relatively infrequent comments generally tend to be poignant.

E: Well, it put my mind at ease today, talking about these things, so it was important to me. I don't know if it was important to him (Frank).

FRANK (F): I'd let you know if it wasn't. (pause)

MT: Well, the way I understand that is, as a couple, you have a need to get some things from us, right? But, you also have some *individual* needs and it sounds like one thing you need, and you said it well, is that you want a set of good parents to tell you that you're okay.

E: Right.

MT: And you seem to need that and that's one function we serve.

E: I think I've needed it less as time goes along, but then when you're way down at the bottom and starting up, I think you need a push to help you get going.

The "reparenting" and other growth-inducing aspects of therapy eventually helped Ellen to formulate an "adult" self less dependent on continual feedback from others. She resumed her education and became an outstanding student. The time demands of her education put some strain on the family, but Frank was able to help out in this regard. The marital relationship became less parentlike, as had been formerly the case, where each spouse (taking over the role of their respective fathers) frequently sat in judgment over the other's shortcomings. A more mutual give-and-take was established, each spouse becoming able to be dependent on the other at times without having to feel "like a naughty child."

The case of Ellen and Frank also illustrates some of the unfinished business from their families of origin that dual-career couples (and perhaps all couples) usually need to work through in the process of assuming comfortable adult and marital roles. Much of the competitive feelings and power conflicts elaborated in previous chapters have their prototypic origins in earlier experiences. For example, competitive feelings often appear to re-create an earlier sibling rivalry. Power struggles may hark back to the helplessness a child feels because he or she is so dependent on powerful adults (parents).

These earlier conflicts and vulnerabilities are especially troubling to dual-career couples, because a large part of their daily lives, particularly their careers, is usually characterized by strong demands for responsible, adult functioning. Co-therapists who are comfortable in interaction with each other can also model a capacity to "play" (often through the use of humor). This behavior can show the couple that upon reaching adulthood one does not completely "put away childish things." Thus, the modeling of a healthy regression in the service of the ego by perceived adult figures (the therapists) can be therapeutically beneficial.

It is important to remember that the co-therapists also have a relationship and that any stresses and strains in their interaction may be picked up by the couple and perhaps exploited by the spouses to the detriment of therapy. Perceived differential status between the co-therapists is a frequent example of this (Rice and Rice, 1975).

Frank and Ellen were the first couple that the co-therapists had treated together, although each therapist had a good deal of prior experience working with other co-therapists. As noted before, there was a tendency initially for Frank and Ellen both to overvalue the male therapist and undervalue the female therapist. Had the co-therapists themselves not been aware of this phenomenon, or if they had reinforced it—e.g., by the male therapist providing most of the "interpretations" and the female therapist most of the "support"—the co-therapy situation could have easily, and perhaps unproductively in the sense of reinforcing fixed roles, recreated to some degree the earlier family situation for both spouses. In this case, the co-therapists quickly became aware of the spouses' attempts to "split" them (divide and conquer) and could comfortably talk about a strategy for coping with this. Over the course of treatment, the co-therapists attempted to reinforce carefully one another's cognitive *and* affective contributions and tried to balance their activity level in a manner that modeled for the couple a more comfortable, egalitarian relationship between two professionals.

In summary, a co-therapy treatment format can be helpful with dual-career couples: (a) if this is requested and preferred by the couple, and (b) if the partners are willing to bear the usual added financial cost of co-therapy. Apart from the rationale that presenting a comfortable two-professional interaction model for dual-career couples can be therapeutic, it should be remembered that co-therapy has not been shown empirically to produce more effective outcomes than treatment with one therapist.

"INDIVIDUAL" VERSUS "COUPLE" THERAPY FOCUS

Throughout this volume, there have been many illustrations of the necessity for taking into account developmental, historical determinants of each spouse's present behavior. These "individual" factors have been seen as coloring the current marital interaction picture in important ways. The author has portrayed many individuals who enter a dual-career marriage as somewhat rigid in personality style. Such spouses are seen as having strong achievement needs that are likely to be long-standing in duration and well reinforced by parents and others. They generally employ cognitive, verbal defenses primarily when faced with the arousal of uncomfortable feelings.

Although this is admittedly a "straw person" portrayal of the type of individual likely to enter a dual-career marriage, the general personality picture is frequently one with strong characterological components. The issue is, therefore, sometimes raised as to whether individual therapy for each spouse should be the treatment of choice. This would be aimed at "loosening up" the personality structure and might be a necessary prerequisite, or at least a helpful adjunctive procedure, of any marital therapy. Even professionals with a strong identity as "marital therapists" may advocate individual therapy at times. For example, Sager (1976) states:

> When the primary conflict is due to neurotic factors in one or both mates that cannot be effectively handled in couple therapy, individual treatment may be indicated, with a return to couple therapy when the threshhold of the neurotic reaction has been raised. Conflicts cannot be reconciled easily when they are intransigent manifestations of opposing biological and intrapsychic needs; when either partner is severely mentally ill; or when conflicts are rooted in a significant difference in intelligence between the partners. Other . . . conflicts that cannot be dealt with adequately in couple therapy include the question of sexual attraction—why one person, as opposed to another, is found sexually attractive—and the problem created by the cessation of previously intense sexual feelings for a partner. (p. 179)

Unfortunately, Sager does not elaborate fully why individual therapy is the treatment of choice in the above instances. Presumably, the anxiety aroused in one spouse by the severely disturbed behavior of the other could be detrimental for marital therapy. In the examples from the sexual arena, perhaps the need is to protect one partner's ego against too great a narcissistic or self-esteem injury, resulting from "honest" sexual revelations by the other.

It is not uncommon for marital therapists to see each spouse separately for *one* session as a part of the intake and diagnostic formulation process at the beginning of therapy. However, even this delineated procedure leaves the therapist vulnerable to hearing "secrets." Knowing such material can lead to a collusion between the therapist and that particular spouse in terms of a "conspiracy of silence" against the other partner. This process can make the therapist uncomfortable about his or her secret knowledge. For this reason, many marital therapists prefer to see the couple conjointly throughout the course of treatment. If the therapist is curious about whether "secrets" are important for understanding the couple's present situation, these can be inquired about directly from each spouse. If such material is revealed (e.g., an affair), it can be dealt with in therapy much like any other "sensitive" revelation.

There seems little rationale for seeing dual-career spouses separately in individual therapy, if their expressed therapy goal is to improve their marriage. A review of marital therapy outcome studies (Gurman and Kniskern, 1978) suggests a conjoint treatment format generally produces more favorable results for the marriage. The fact that individuals in a dual-career partnership often have similar personality traits and patterns means that "individual work" with one partner by the therapist, relating background and developmental experiences to current conflicts, will likely have some meaning for the other spouse. In any case, it would seem important that both spouses be a part of this learning process, so that they might each better understand where the other is "coming from." The need for special ego protection (e.g., in regard to past or present affairs or other "secrets") is often not an overriding consideration with dual-career couples. Such individuals commonly have at least a modicum of ego strength, and this has often been shown by their educational and occupational perseverance as well as by their tolerance for stress both in school and on the job.

The one exception to seeing the couple conjointly occurs in the case of couples who have made a decision to separate and/or to divorce. Such individuals may wish help with the psychological process of separating as well as for certain practical issues, e.g., minimizing the stress of the separation for their children, or establishing communication sufficient to reach satisfactory economic and/or custody arrangements.

The author has found a structured separation with counseling procedure (Toomin, 1972) to be useful for many such couples, particularly if they have already made the decision to dissolve their relationship. In this treatment format, after agreeing to live apart, the couple is seen together for periodic conjoint sessions. These are usually interspersed with individual sessions for each partner. A total treatment period of ten to fifteen meetings is most frequently arranged. In this treatment format, the combination of individual and couple sessions mirrors the phenomenology of each spouse's current situation. They are still together in some ways, but apart in others.

The author's experience is that dual-career couples may on the average show slightly less psychological trauma when ending their marriage than couples in a more traditional marriage. The ability to "escape" into one's work, mentioned previously, and each spouse's relative financial independence make the psychological process of separating a little easier. This is particularly true if the couple does not have children. When children are involved, increased psychological stress is normally engendered and the psychological process is often more difficult. However, Toomin (1972) reports that the structured separation procedure, while not substantially "saving" couples from divorce, did facilitate a smoother working out of child support and custody arrangements.

TREATMENT OF DUAL-CAREER COUPLES—A SUMMARY

The author has reviewed general marital therapy treatment considerations with dual-career couples, as well as elaborating several "core" conflicts and additional treatment issues. A summary of certain personality attributes of dual-career partners and typical characteristics of their marital interaction is presented below. This is organized in terms of facilitative and complicating factors for marital treatment. As little has been written previously about working therapeutically with dual-career couples, the listing below is based primarily on the author's experience.

Dual-career couples who have shown a positive response to therapy appear to be characterized by one or more of the following:

1. A freedom from rigidly prescribed gender role behaviors and constraints.

2. A flexibility and willingness to try new behaviors, including those that involve some risk (in the sense that their implementation is likely to change the relationship).

3. A willingness to share power or influence in the relationship and an appreciation of the destructive, as well as the facilitative, effects of competition.

4. A valuing of affective communication and openness to one's own and one's partner's feelings.

5. An appreciation of each partner's right to self-fulfillment and a willingness to make some sacrifices in this regard. A component of this attitude is often a relative freedom from jealousy and possessiveness.

Those dual-career couples who have not shown substantial improvement with marital therapy have typically manifested one or more of the following characteristics:

1. Strong rigidity and inflexibility around the possibility of change, particularly in regard to gender-role stereotyped behaviors.

2. An unwillingness to risk and try new, potentially innovative solutions to situations of stalemate in the marriage (e.g., the acceptance of a mutually unsatisfying sexual relationship).

3. A readiness to escape into their respective careers for satisfaction rather than working toward a balance of occupational and marital gratification.

4. An inability to separate from their families of origin in order to more fully participate in evolving an alternative (to the "traditional") marital life-style.

5. An inability to share power or influence within the marital relationship, along with its common accompaniment, destructive interspouse competition.

Marital therapists will recognize many of the above as applicable to treatment with couples in general. However, the dual-career life-style is likely to introduce certain specific variants of each factor and these have been the focus here.

·10·

Optimizing the Dual-Career Life-Style

Case #14. Tom, age 44, and Nancy, age 37, have been married for thirteen years. They are the parents of Carolyn, age 11, and Ben, age 8. Tom works as a research scientist for an aerospace company and Nancy is an occupational therapist in a large metropolitan hospital. They have lived for ten years in a pleasant suburban neighborhood where they are both fairly active in community and school affairs. Their marriage, after some initial rough spots, has acquired a comfortableness which seems to be based, in part, on a sense of a sustaining commitment.

Nancy is the oldest of two daughters. Her sister, Lisa, is two years younger. Lisa is married to an insurance executive and the couple has three children. Lisa is not employed outside the home, although she is active in local political campaigns. Lisa lives in a large city about two hundred miles away from Nancy. The sisters see each other several times a year, usually at holidays, and occasionally for a weekend in the summer.

Nancy's father died of cancer six years before at the age of 63. Her mother (age 66) lives in a suburb not too far from where Lisa and her family live. Nancy's father owned a furniture store and her mother worked in the store part time as a bookkeeper during the time the girls were growing up. The family was comfortable financially. They were a fairly close-knit group, and hard work was emphasized. Her father's family had come to America from northern Europe in the late 1920s. They had just settled in when the Depression hit, and Nancy's father recalled very hard times for his family during that period. Out of this experience came a resolve to work hard and to provide his own family with economic security. Although much of the family's life revolved around the furniture store, Nancy can recall a general feeling of harmony and cooperation in the family. She experienced her parents as accessible and remembers with particular fondness annual summer vacations to the ocean, where the family rented a cottage for several weeks.

Nancy felt her parents expected a good deal of maturity on her part. She was expected to be responsible for Lisa during periods when both her parents were at the store. This began when Nancy was 11 and continued until she was about 16. Nancy recalls that she and her sister differed in temperament. Nancy was more socially reserved than Lisa and spent more of her time at home reading. She enjoyed being a teen volunteer at a local hospital, where she delivered books and magazines to patients and was able to spend a fair amount of time talking with them. She describes Lisa as more interested in dating, high school sports and other school-related extracurricular activities.

Nancy began dating when she was 16, during her sophomore year in high school. She did not date extensively during high school or early college. She had her first serious relationship during her junior year in college with Jerry, who was a senior. There was some brief talk of possibly getting married, but this notion dissipated when Jerry decided to go to graduate school in a distant city. Nancy liked her college and realized she wanted to spend her senior year there. Despite mutual spoken wishes to maintain the relationship, Nancy and Jerry drifted apart during her senior year. The relationship had been a relatively smooth one and was her first sexual experience. She realizes in retrospect that differences in their backgrounds would likely have caused problems over time. Jerry came from a relatively poor farm family and had a different religious background than Nancy.

Tom is the oldest of three children. He has a brother, who is married, has one child, and works as an engineer, and a sister, who is divorced and has two children. Both his siblings are several years younger than Tom. Tom's parents are both deceased. His father was a civil engineer and his mother was not employed outside the home. Tom's father died four years earlier and his mother died during the past year. Tom recalls that his father was a shy person, who conveyed a sense of caring for his family, but rarely showed his feelings openly. Tom was closer emotionally to his mother than to his father. The main area of common interest for Tom and his father was in building and constructing projects, and in repairing things around the house. However, once his father showed him how things were to be done, Tom stated, "We worked pretty much in silence." He had some sense that his father carried a fair amount of inner pain, but he did not know the genesis of this. He recalls that his father was periodically depressed. His parents' marriage did not seem like a particularly happy one, even though Tom cannot recall the issue of divorce ever having been discussed.

Tom dated little in high school, where he was active in science activities and was on the swimming team. He went to a few dances and school social gatherings, but generally did not feel particularly comfortable in dating relationships. In college, he dated more frequently and joined a fraternity, which provided a ready social milieu. His first serious relationship (with Donna) lasted for one and a half years, beginning during the second semester of her junior year. Donna was an art major and was more openly expressive of feelings than Tom, a quality which attracted him to her. She liked his sense of emotional "evenness" and admired his scientific curiosity. Over time, differences in temperament began to cause friction in the relationship, which ended by mutual agreement when Donna graduated. Tom recalls: "I think it had been over for some time, but neither of us wanted to hurt the other by calling it quits."

Tom and Nancy met at the house of one of her colleagues, whose husband knew Tom. The wife had invited them both and introduced them in a kidding manner with the remark: "I've been thinking it's time both of you found somebody." At the time of their meeting, Tom was 30 years old and Nancy was 23. He had a well established position as head of the research division for a small technical company, and she was in her first year as an occupational therapist in a children's hospital. Tom had felt increasingly unhappy with his limited social life and had begun a pattern of periodically drinking to excess. This caused some concern among his friends. He acknowledged that drinking has eased the pain of his loneliness, but brushed off concern of friends by saying: "Well, I always make it to work, don't I?"

Both Nancy and Tom were put off by the directness of her friend's effort at matchmaking. Following the evening when they met, a month elapsed before Tom decided that he would like to get to know Nancy better. They went out to dinner and subsequently began dating on a frequent basis. She was worried about his drinking (to which she had been alerted by her friend's husband), but this did not become a serious problem, as his alcohol abuse subsided rapidly once their relationship intensified.

Nancy was attracted to a gentle quality in Tom's personality. She appreciated his patience and perseverance. She entered the relationship thinking that their age difference (seven years) would probably preclude developing any permanent relationship. He found himself opening up rather soon to Nancy, in a way that surprised him. He found her easy to talk with and she conveyed a genuine interest in his life and work. (There appeared to be a strong, subconscious attraction to one another based on Tom's need to be rescued from his loneliness and Nancy's need to feel vitally needed by someone who needed her help. She felt she was ready to settle down and the idea of marrying a responsible, mature man, who might wish to begin a family soon after marriage, appealed to her from early in the relationship.)

The couple married after a year of courtship. Nancy had made it clear that she found a good deal of satisfaction in her career and that she expected to work, at least half time, even when the couple had young children. Tom supported Nancy's career ambitions and admired her dedication. At the end of the second year of marriage (when Carolyn was approximately four months old), Tom left the small company where he had been working to take a laboratory research position with his present, larger company. The position offered him greater time flexibility and more of a chance to "do my own thing." The company had a flex-time system that permitted Tom to begin work later in the morning and continue past the usual quitting time. This meant he could stay home in the morning for a while with Carolyn (and, later, with Ben) while Nancy went to work. She would then pick up the children at their regular sitter's house and be with them in the late afternoon.

Clearly, Tom enjoyed the children and felt that having a family had enabled him to overcome his loneliness and the pain of his former social isolation. (Significant in this is Tom's identification with his father's periodic depressions and marital dissatisfaction. Tom had been uncertain in his late twenties as to whether he would ever get married. In some ways, he had been rather unsuccessfully, at least from a psychological happiness standpoint, preparing himself for bachelorhood.) Having established himself professionally, and having a relatively undemanding job, Tom felt greater freedom to spend time with Nancy and his children. Like Nancy, he had taken care of his younger siblings on occasion while he was growing up. This seemed instrumental in freeing him from hangups about a man taking care of small children and sharing domestic responsibilities. Tom and Nancy operate on an informal domestic and child-care task schedule, but there is a lot of "doing whatever needs to be done by whoever is around when it needs doing." There is a sense of cooperation between the partners in this regard and the indication of a fair amount of good will in the relationship is evident to the outside observer. Nancy will usually stay home when Ben or Carolyn is sick, and this seems to have been determined by the fact that she, more easily than Tom, can get a fellow worker to cover for her on the job.

The couple's social relationships are limited to a few close friends whom they see periodically. Almost all their friends are couples where one of the partners is a colleague of Tom's or Nancy's. They do not find these social relationships particularly gratifying and are likely to entertain primarily to reciprocate prior invitations or to fulfill work-connected obligations (e.g., entertaining the boss once or twice a year). Tom and Nancy prefer to spend their leisure time with the family. They have recently begun to build a small cabin on some wooded land they purchased several years ago. This has become a regular and rewarding weekend project.

Although both describe their relationship as "happy" and generally fulfilling of each other's intimacy needs, the marriage has not been conflict-free. Both partners were used to being on their own at the time of their marriage. Having to share space with someone else, and having to give up some of the personal autonomy each had felt previously, resulted in a fair amount of ambivalent feelings early in the relationship. Neither partner is comfortable with expressing anger directly, and it takes a fair amount of time and provocation before such feelings are revealed openly. The result of this process is that both Tom and Nancy have felt at times like "we could never really resolve anything." Their sexual relationship had been a relatively comfortable one, though it has become somewhat routine and predictable. Neither partner seems troubled enough by this, at present, to wish to attempt any major change in their pattern of sexual interaction.

The early difficulties in the marriage generally disappeared after Carolyn's birth. This event appears to have served to cement their commitment to the relationship, and, indeed, the wish to secure this may have led to the decision to have a child soon after marrying. The timing of their second child (three years later) was determined largely by Nancy's desire to continue working and not to be physically drained "by having two children in diapers at the same time."

Currently, Tom is feeling some aspects of a midlife crisis. He worries on occasion that he may be "over the hill" in terms of his research creativity. He finds himself somewhat less rewarded in his profession, particularly when compared to the gratification obtained from his family. He is questioning the proper balance between these two areas of his life. He is also more sensitive recently to the age difference between himself and Nancy. Partly in response to the methodical character of their sexual relationship, he worries that she may be attracted to another (younger) man, although he shares these fears with her and she tells him "not to worry."

Nancy feels ambivalent about their decision not to have any more children. She feels less needed as Ben gets older and is better able to care for himself. The comfortable and predictable nature of their lives is both reassuring and troubling. She wonders, on occasion, if there are any big changes in store for them that would bring excitement and intensity into the relationship. She muses to herself what it would be like to have an affair (and perhaps communicates this unconsciously to Tom, feeding his fears about the possibility of this happening). However, she does not actively pursue the translating of such fantasies into actual behavior.

Recently, the couple had decided that it would be a good idea to take a vacation by themselves, leaving the children for a week with friends. This represents a new travel format, as all prior extended vacations have been taken with the whole family. In planning for this, there is a sense that the marital relationship needs some intensification and renewal.

In summary, Tom and Nancy are representative of many (perhaps most) dual-career couples, who find this marital life-style generally satisfying. Neither partner feels he or she must make disproportionate sacrifices in order to have a career and a family.

They have maintained a flexibility in dealing with the demands placed on their lives and show a relative freedom from gender-role stereotyped notions of what is and is not "proper" spouse behavior. Tom and Nancy have a sense of how to promote renewal and revitalization in their relationship in order to escape boredom and cope with routine. Although not free of problems, they are motivated to work on rough spots and attempt to keep channels of communication open. While this couple is not typical of spouses seen in a marital therapy practice, they do offer a useful model of how at least one dual-career couple is able to make their relationship "work."

As previously documented (Chapter 2), large numbers of couples have only recently opted for a dual-career marital lifestyle. The lack of readily available role models has necessitated a flexibility and willingness to experiment with solutions to dual-career marital problems. The next generation of dual-career families seems likely to benefit from this process.

It is important to keep in mind that, despite the high degree of stress experienced in dual-career families, on the whole such couples (like Tom and Nancy) report a high degree of marital satisfaction (Rapoport and Rapoport, 1971; Johnson and Johnson, 1977; Staines, Pleck, Shepard and O'Connor, 1978; St. John-Parsons, 1978). The excitement and challenge in this type of marital arrangement generally appear to outweigh the exhaustion, relationship time limitations, and diminished social life, both with friends and family, commonly reported in studies of such couples. There are also no indications in the literature that children of dual-career couples are, as a group, affected adversely by being in a dual-career family. There is an emphasis on the children being somewhat independent, responsible and resourceful (Rapoport and Rapoport, 1971; Johnson and Johnson, 1977; St. John-Parsons, 1978), but they are usually seemingly happy and adjusted. Perceived family satisfaction may improve as the children get older, with younger children producing disproportionately greater role strain, particularly for dual-career wives (Staines, Pleck, Shepard and O'Connor, 1978).

Implementation of this alternative marital life-style has been hindered by the inevitable slow process of social change. For example, the United States is the only major industrialized western country that lacks a state run and subsidized system of day care for children (Horton, 1971). Although many dual-career families might not avail themselves of such a setup, it could serve at times as a helpful backup support system. In addition, the inflexibility of the occupational structure—e.g., the limited availability of part-time positions—has worked against many dual-career couples' attempts to balance the conflicting demands of home, family and work (Holmstrom, 1972).

If only for economic reasons, leaving aside the wish for self-fulfillment, an increasing number of couples seem destined to choose a dual-career marital arrangement. Research studies are only beginning to collect data on how the personal and marital fulfillment of such individuals can be enhanced. In a pioneering investigation, Gronseth (1975, discussed in Rapoport and Rapoport, 1976, pp. 340–343) studied 28 Norwegian families. Sixteen of these had adopted a "work-sharing" pattern whereby each spouse did 50% of the work in the family. This meant a total sharing of *all* domestic and child-care tasks, including those traditionally assigned to the spouse of the opposite gender. Gronseth included seven additional families who wished to adopt this pattern but could not find employment that would permit them to do so, and five "traditional" families who served as a small control group.

Gronseth found most of the wives, who, like their husbands, came from predominantly middle-class backgrounds, had strong occupational *and* familial commitments. Most of the wives were not employed in professional level careers. The husbands respected their wives' commitments and held for themselves either somewhat anticareer or "moderated" career ambitions. Both spouses' main motivation in adopting the work-sharing pattern was to be able to share in the active rearing of their children.

Gronseth indicates that 7 of the 16 couples (43.75%) were able to attain very close to a fifty-fifty sharing of tasks. Achieving this was facilitated by the following factors: (a) the wives' high educational attainment, (b) the wives' access to productive and satisfying employment, (c) a definite but moderate level of work commitment on the wives' part, (d) the familistic and relatively non-careerist orientation of the husbands, and (e) child-centered attitudes and orientation on the part of both spouses. All the couples in the work-sharing group felt an enrichment of their life experience and increased common interests as a result of this arrangement. Roughly one-fourth of the couples reported an improvement in their sexual relationship, compared to the time before they adopted the work-sharing pattern. (This may in part have been a result of their being home more and spending a greater amount of time together during the week.)

In summary, the Gronseth study suggests an innovative way couples can arrange for both spouses to combine family and career interests and tasks. This can be possible only if there is flexibility in the occupational system to allow for part-time work, with the provision of comparable job benefits. At present, it is common in the United States and many other countries for less than full-time work to have a greater than proportionate reduction in fringe benefits.

The work-sharing pattern can obviate many of the difficulties faced by dual-career couples when both spouses work full time, e.g., the limited amount of time such individuals report they have to be together as a couple. Work-sharing does, of course, reduce the economic advantage of having both spouses' combined full-time incomes and, for this reason alone, may not meet with ready acceptance by a large number of dual-career couples. In addition, work sharing requires an unusual freedom from the constraints of gender-role conditioning and domestic "territoriality" on the part of both partners. Dual-career couples have usually shown some flexibility in this area, with the resultant felt freedom to choose domestic and child-care tasks based on competence and preference rather than prescription. In this regard, they are not that far from implementing a work-sharing pattern and may perhaps increasingly do so in the future, being willing to trade off the economic limitations for familial and relationship benefits.

The work-sharing pattern is but one example of creative solutions likely to be needed by such couples in optimizing their dual-career marriage. The high level of satisfaction (even in the face of heightened stress) felt by many dual-career couples attests to the potential benefits to be gained if they are able to work through marital problems and conflicts. An awareness on the marital therapist's part of typical conflict areas and strategies for coping with them will hopefully facilitate helping dual-career couples who enter marital therapy. This awareness, plus a relative freedom from bias and an openness to nontraditional marital life-styles, can work to the mutual benefit of the therapist and the couple.

· Appendix ·

Extended Case Study: Therapy with a Dual-Career Couple

A MORE SYSTEMATIC VIEW of how a therapist might handle representative conflicts encountered by dual-career couples is presented below in an extended case study. The issues of competition, shared control and arranging a support system highlighted in this volume were all dealt with in the course of treatment with this particular couple. The partners were seen a total of fourteen sessions. The wife, who initiated contact with the therapist, complaining of career dissatisfaction, was seen alone first. All the remaining sessions were conjoint, i.e., both partners were present with the therapist.

Case #15 Roger (age 36) and Sharon (age 35) have been married for twelve years and have two children, Pam, 9, and Doug, 5. They live in a small university town, where Roger is a professor in the humanities and Sharon holds a responsible position in the university administration. They have lived in their present location for seven years, having moved there after Roger completed his graduate work.

Sharon was referred to the therapist by her family doctor. A routine physical had picked up evidence of mild hypertension. Her blood pressure had been in the normal range in prior exams. The internist inquired whether Sharon could relate any stress or change in her life to the rise in her blood pressure. She responded by admitting that she felt a good deal of pressure on her job. As a midlevel administrator, she was caught between the demands of students, toward whom she was generally sympathetic, and the directives of her superiors, toward whom she often felt ambivalence. This bind left her at times both depressed and anxious.

Recently, she had been thinking of resigning her job and returning to school in order to complete her doctorate in education.

At the end of the physical exam, Sharon's physician raised the possibility of referral to a psychotherapist, in order to help her more fully explore the stress in her life and, hopefully, increase her ability to cope with it. She accepted the referral and initiated contact with one of the therapists whose names had been given to her by the internist.

Sharon came alone to the first therapy session. She was dressed attractively and casually. She was generally neat in appearance, of average height, and somewhat on the thin side. She stated that she was nervous "about being in a shrink's office" and fidgeted during much of the interview. She clearly saw the feelings of job dissatisfaction as basically "my problem." When the therapist inquired as to how her husband was reacting to all this, Sharon replied: "Well, we don't talk about it a lot. Roger has his own problems with his work. He's very conscientious about his teaching and he's always giving time to help his students—they really seem to appreciate it." Sharon's answer suggested to the therapist that she might be feeling some lack of support from Roger and that this could be exacerbating her reaction to her job situation. The therapist suggested: "I'd really like to get Roger's perspective on all this. Do you think he'd be willing to come in with you next time?" Sharon responded: "I don't know why not. I think he's a little worried about me. He was really surprised when he asked about how my physical went and I told him my blood pressure was up. He's used to seeing me around the house, where I'm more easygoing." She agreed to ask Roger to come in and the rest of the session was spent in taking a developmental, social and family history.

Sharon is the youngest of two children in her family. She has a brother, Steven, two years older, who is a journalist and lives several hundred miles away. Steven is separated from his wife, and the couple has three children. Sharon indicated that a possible reconciliation was in the offing. Sharon's father, age 63, is employed as an accountant by the government and her mother, also 63, is not currently employed, although for most of her life she was a music teacher. Seasonal arthritis forced her to quit teaching about three years ago.

Sharon grew up in a suburb (population approximately 35,000) of a large metropolitan city. She remembers having a lot of friends until about the age of 12. There were the usual sibling squabbles with Steven, except that their parents generally intervened quickly to stop such bickering. As her mother gave music lessons in the home during the late afternoons, there was an emphasis on the maintenance of decorum, particularly at those times. Sharon grew up in a temperate climate and remembers preferring to be outside a great deal of the time "rather than inside listening to all that banging on the piano." Most of her neighborhood friends during childhood were boys, and she remembers herself as "something of a tomboy." She recalls: "I'd climb trees right along with the guys. They had built a treehouse and I was the only girl in the neighborhood willing to climb up to it. The boys must have been impressed with that because they let me in (the treehouse) despite all the cracks about 'yucky girls.' " It also seemed clear that Steven helped somewhat to smooth the way for her acceptance by the boys in the neighborhood.

The family was fairly religious (Protestant), and Sharon remembers from a young age going to church and Sunday school. Going to church seemed to have been mainly a social experience for her. The religious teachings, however, did serve to emphasize self-control and reinforced to a certain extent the emphasis at home placed on the control of strong feelings.

She remembers her family life as generally pleasant and somewhat uneventful. Her mother began teaching her the piano at age 6 and this continued until she was around 13. She enjoyed music and remembers warmly her mother's special attention to her in this area. She felt somewhat more distant from her father, who often worked at home in the evenings and "seemed to prefer being with Steven anyway." She continued: "I'm not sure he ever understood girls; in a way, he turned me over to Mom to raise." It was clear, however, that both parents were very interested in their children's academic performance, e.g., rewarding them monetarily for good grades.

The family's social life was not extensive and their occasional social contacts were generally with friends met through church-related activities. The family took two weeks' vacation each summer, and this was typically spent in seeing different parts of the country. Sharon's father was a history buff, and the vacations were often planned so as to include visiting several sites of historical importance.

Sharon remembers an important change in her life that oc-

155

curred around age 13. This was approximately a year after puberty began. She reports starting to feel uncomfortable with her childhood friends and began a period of mild social withdrawal which lasted until her senior year of high school. Since she had played mostly with boys when growing up, the distancing from these relationships left her with few friends. She did develop a close relationship with one girlfriend, Sue, during her early and middle teens, but she remembers feeling lonely and socially isolated during this period. She read a great deal, getting into romantic fantasies and picturing herself as a historical figure during different centuries.

To the therapist, Sharon's withdrawal during her teens seemed additionally related to her increasing sexual awareness. The religious and familial attitude toward sex was generally repressive. There had been some early exploratory sex play on two occasions with one of the boys in the neighborhood, but Sharon felt guilty about this and refused his and other boys' further requests for similar interactions. She did not tell her parents about these early episodes, stating: "That sort of thing just wasn't talked about at home. I learned about it mostly at school and Sue filled in the details." Sharon indicated that her mother was openly and spontaneously affectionate with her and with Steven, but noted: "I saw very little of that going on between Mom and Dad. I guess they did it. I mean, they slept in the same bed and they had two kids."

Sharon had a few ritual dates (Christmas dance, Junior Prom) in her first three years of high school. She stated: "I felt comfortable with guys, but it was different than before (in her childhood relationships)." To the therapist, Sharon's delay in actively pursuing heterosexual relationships seemed related, in addition, to perhaps a greater than average degree of sexual identity conflict. Her "tomboy period" had been exciting and involving, and her generally repressive social conditioning had left her with little felt freedom to explore and discover herself as a sexual woman.

During her senior year, Sharon began dating a young man, Dan, who was a year older than she, and was in his first year at a community college in the town where she lived. Dan was very interested in literature and saw himself as an aspiring writer. Dan had met Sharon's brother, Steven, in a pickup basketball game, and they had become friends. Steven introduced him to Sharon and the two felt an immediate attraction. They dated for about a year, until Sharon went away to college. In many ways, this first love was a tangible extension of many of the fantasies engendered by her readings during early and middle adolescence. There was strong mutual physical attraction, but she maintained a "technical virginity," setting limits on their ardor by refusing to have intercourse. Nonetheless, her physical and sexual responsiveness was reassuring to her and appeared to signal the start of a somewhat delayed period of sexual identity resolution. The relationship with Dan ended shortly after she began college (at a university several hundred miles away). She was forced to realize the high degree of romantic illusion in their relationship when Dan chose another heroine with whom to play out the next chapter in his literary life. Sharon was hurt by Dan's rejection, but found college stimulating and turned her attention to her academic studies.

Sharon dated a moderate amount during her first two-and-a-half years of college. She met Roger during the last half of her junior year. They were both volunteers at a nursing home and got to know one another during trips from campus out to the home. Driving was arranged according to which one of the several volunteers had a car available on that particular day. After two months of getting to know one another in this manner, Roger asked Sharon if she'd like to go to a movie with him. Subsequently, they began a period of frequent dating that ultimately led to marriage, a few months after graduation.

Sharon was an excellent student throughout her school years. In college, she received much encouragement from several of her teachers to go on to graduate school in her major, comparative literature. She knew from early in high school (where she admired and, to a certain extent, idealized several women teachers) that she wanted a career. She was unsure about future job possibilities in literature, and took several education courses that would enable her to qualify for teaching certification. She found her volunteer work at the nursing home gratifying and began to wonder whether she should go into some field of social service. Sharon toyed with the idea of taking a fifth undergraduate year to pursue additional undergraduate courses that would enable her to go on for a master's degree in social work. However, she finally settled on graduate work in education, feeling that such a choice could combine both her interests in teaching and in helping people.

In summary, Sharon brought to her marriage with Roger strong, well-rewarded intellectual interests and accomplishments.

She had relatively well-formulated career plans and ambitions. She had had only a moderate amount of social and dating experience and limited sexual experience. Many of her ideas about permanent, committed relationships were formulated from her reading of historical novels and the accompanying fantasies. There had been relatively little testing out of her romantic notions within the realities of a long-term relationship. Her one experience along these lines (with Dan) had left her feeling wounded and mildly disillusioned. She recovered from this experience by reinvolving herself in academics, an area where she consistently achieved success.

Roger accompanied Sharon to the second therapy session and the period of marital treatment began. He was of average build, wore glasses and dressed slightly on the modish side. Partly out of a need to explore the marital dynamics, the therapist did not take the time to pursue as careful a developmental, social and family history with Roger as had been done in the first session with Sharon. This handicapped the therapist's understanding of Roger (and of the marital relationship) at times. Occasionally, facts relating to Roger's background were gathered and explored during one of the subsequent therapy sessions, when the material seemed pertinent to the particular issue being dealt with by the couple.

Roger grew up in a moderately large city in the Midwest. His father (age 59) is a skilled craftsman who worked for a large company which manufactures machinery. His grandparents had come over from Europe in their twenties. His mother (age 56) works as an aide in a technical library. She is the more intellectually curious of his parents and has taken university extension courses, completing the equivalent of three years of college. Roger is an only child. Due to physical complications, labor and delivery had been difficult, and his mother was advised not to have any more children. His parents explored the possibility of adopting a second child, but abandoned the idea after Roger's mother decided (when he was 4) that she would like to get a part-time job. The family has several relatives in the same city, and Roger remembers being cared for regularly by an aunt, who has two children of her own, one of them a son who is about Roger's age. He recalls, with fondness, his aunt's house, and states that this was partly because "she knew what little boys were like, and didn't mind it so much (as my mother) if we messed up the house."

Most of the family's social contacts center around their relatives, with whom holidays and other special occasions are shared. The family is Catholic, though not particularly religious, and attends church only for Christmas, Easter, baptisms, confirmations and the like.

Roger remembers his parents as affectionate and expressive of their feelings. They have generally seemed preoccupied, however, with getting to a position of financial stability. For example, money that might have gone into extended vacations is either saved or put into fixing up their home. Roger feels that his mother is more upwardly mobile than his father, and sees her finding a job when he was young as motivated primarily by the wish to improve the family's lot financially. He presents his mother as the more dominant partner, and as a strong-willed person. Father is seen as more easygoing and as a more social person than his mother.

Roger's mother gave him a lot of attention when he was growing up, but appeared to stop short of spoiling him unduly. For example, she encouraged him to get a job during the sixth grade and helped him to secure a paper route. She took him to concerts, art galleries and museums, all dictated according to her wish that he should be a person sensitive to cultural experiences. She helped him with his schoolwork, sometimes gently chiding his father for "letting him play so much."

Roger did well in school and was reasonably popular with playmates. His childhood seems to have proceeded relatively smoothly. He participated in several neighborhood sports but remembers gathering "little of the acclaim given to the boys in the neighborhood who were good athletes." When junior high began, he gave up most of his athletic participation to concentrate on school and his part-time job as a paper carrier.

Roger began dating early in high school and had his first brief sexual experience at age 15 with "the girl in the neighborhood who took personal responsibility for the *rites de passage*." He showed some artistic ability and many of his dating experiences involved girls he became acquainted with in art class. He did not have any extended, serious dating relationship during high school.

In his junior year of high school, Roger decided to attend one of the large universities in his state. In college, he became interested in history and for a time considered art history as a major that would combine two of his strong academic interests. He realized art would best be left as an avocation and settled on history, ultimately earning a doctorate and teaching at the university level in a related area of social science.

Roger joined a small fraternity. It was as a nursing home volunteer, in a fraternity and sorority co-sponsored program, that he met Sharon. He had a serious relationship during his sophomore year with Sue, a woman student his age. They had met in a history class and ultimately lived together for a couple of months or "long enough to find out we weren't going to make it." He continued: "It was my idea to live together and I think I was mainly looking for security. Sue wasn't really ready to make that kind of commitment and wanted to still go out occasionally with other guys. That led to several fights and finally we had to face up to the fact that we were in different places."

In summary, Roger is an only child in an upwardly mobile family dominated by his mother. She spent a good deal of effort on his development, particularly in providing a breadth of cultural experiences. There has been an emphasis placed on his developing responsibility, on hard work, and on achievement. His father is expressive, more social than his mother, and more easygoing. His father has not appeared to play as dominant a role as his mother in Roger's life. His childhood and adolescent developmental progression was generally without psychological trauma and included an average amount of dating and other social relationship experience.

Excerpts are presented below from the fourteen couple therapy sessions with Roger and Sharon. In the original session, with only Sharon present, the therapist had developed a hypothesis that the felt lack of emotional support from Roger was contributing to the stress she was feeling in her life. This hypothesis was explored in the first couple therapy session. The therapist was also initially sensitive to the issue of whether Roger might already have perceived an alliance between Sharon and the therapist, based on the prior session. There seemed little evidence of this in the early sessions. If there had been indications of such a potentially dysfunctional perceived alliance, the therapist would have suggested bringing in a co-therapist. The co-therapy format could have given Roger the opportunity of having an "ally" in the sessions. As it turned out, a co-therapist did not appear to be needed.

SESSION #1

The first part of the hour was devoted to establishing rapport with Roger and finding out what Sharon had told him about the original therapy session. Roger's initial attitude was clearly that Sharon was the "identified patient" (the one with the problems). He stated: "I'm here to help (her) in any way I can." He was friendly toward the therapist and generally nondefensive when discussing himself.

At this point (about twenty minutes into the session), it is not clear whether Roger will be present at future sessions, since the problems being presented by Sharon have not yet been defined as "marital problems." Therefore, the therapist decides that he needs to get Roger's perspective on how he perceives Sharon and their marital relationship. Even if Roger does not continue, this information is important for filling out the therapist's knowledge of the couple's relationship history.

The therapist introduces the subject of the marriage:

THERAPIST (T): I'd be interested in how you two got together. I understand from Sharon that you met while you were in college and both were volunteers at a nursing home. But I'd really like to know what attracted you to one another.

ROGER (R): (smiling a little sheepishly) Well, she was more serious about things than most of the girls I had met. We seemed to be able to talk pretty easily and she'd read widely. Almost any book I'd read she'd read, too. . . . All that, plus she's not bad looking (looks at Sharon; she smiles in return). That's helpful.

T: I see. (to Sharon) How about you?

SHARON (S): I agree with what he said. He liked historical biography, which I liked to read, too. We could both envision living in different times. He was more open about his feelings than other guys I'd known and I liked that.

T: How about the eventual decision to get married? How was that made?

S: We dated for a year and a half. Roger wanted to live together for a while but I didn't feel quite right about that. After graduation, Roger had a commitment to working in a summer camp, where he'd been a counselor before. He finished in the middle of August and we got married after that.

T: Were you at the summer camp too?

S: No, we were apart for about two months. I stayed on campus and worked in the library. We saw each other about once every three weeks.

R: (interrupting) In a way, it was kind of a test, about whether we really wanted to get married.

T: (gently) Why did you feel the need for a test?

R: I'm not sure. (Sharon nods agreement.)

Significant to the therapist in this regard was the later revelation by Roger that he had been rejected by a woman in his one prior serious relationship. Sharon had a similar history of feeling wounded in her one important prior relationship with a man. The testing period during the summer immediately before their marriage may have been an attempt to make sure that the relationship bonding was strong enough to withstand the adversity of separation. The script for the courtship and early years of their marriage was a strongly romantic one. In this sense, testing their love by being apart and feeling it strengthened served as proof of the "rightness" of their having chosen one another for marital partners.

The couple entered graduate school together shortly after marriage and a brief honeymoon (which apparently did not include visiting any historical sites). Both Roger and Sharon were involved in their demanding academic work and, aside from the usual adjustments to the experience of living together for the first time, it was a relatively smooth period. Roger was more comfortable sexually than Sharon. This seemed the result both of his greater sexual experience and his less psychologically repressive background. She reports that he was usually patient and gentle as a lover. As she learned to relax, Sharon became increasingly sexually responsive and generally began to reach orgasm during intercourse toward the end of the first year of marriage.

Sharon received her master's degree at the end of her second year of graduate work. She thought of continuing on for her doctorate, but decided against it partly because she and Roger had begun to talk about starting a family in the not-too-distant future. Sharon felt that being full time in graduate school and having a

162

young child would be too demanding of her time and energy. She took a job working in the office of one of the university administrators as a coordinator of educational programs. She had done a field placement in the same office, and had liked working there. They had been pleased with her work, and this led to the job offer.

Sharon had discussed with her boss the possibility of working part time, if and when she had children, and he seemed open to negotiating this. As it turned out, she became pregnant after approximately thirteen months of trying, and Pam was born at the end of Sharon's second year of work. She found it difficult to return to work (after two months) on a half-time basis, as she had been very involved in her job, and it was hard to give what she perceived as less than a full-time effort.

Roger progressed in his graduate work, although his dissertation took longer than he had anticipated. It was a while before he was able to settle on a topic that gained his dissertation committee's agreement. Following the selection of a topic, there was the inevitable difficulty of pleasing the several "masters" on his committee throughout the course of the dissertation. After his fifth year of graduate work, with the dissertation about two-thirds completed, Roger took a job at the university where he is presently teaching. Sharon was apprehensive about the move, but agreed with Roger that he needed to get started in his professional career. Fortunately, contacts between her boss and university administrators at the new location landed a similar part-time job for her. Roger completed his dissertation at the end of his first semester of teaching and was given a promotion, from instructor to assistant professor.

The couple bought a house with down-payment money frugally saved from Sharon's job. She anticipated that Roger would have more time for home and family with the burden of the dissertation lifted from his shoulders. Unfortunately, that wish did not come true. He went from the pressure of the dissertation to the pressure of being on a tenure track appointment, with its demands for scholarly productivity. Sharon felt increasing disappointment over Roger's lack of attention to the family. She did not express these feelings openly, in part because she realized that it was important for Roger to establish himself professionally. She busied herself with the details of fixing up the new house and learning her new job. Roger, though limited in the time he felt able to spend with Pam, seemed to enjoy his daughter (now almost 3 years old), and that was comforting to Sharon.

At this point, the first hint of future trouble for the marriage occurred. Sharon seemed aware that she was being asked to make certain sacrifices (e.g., to work half time, do more of the child care, and handle most of the day-to-day domestic tasks), but chose to ignore the small resentments engendered by these circumstances. In a slow and somewhat insidious way, the marriage was falling into a more traditional pattern. Roger expected that his career would be facilitated by Sharon's freeing him from domestic and child-care responsibilities. As she was "only working half time," there was a subtle agreement by both partners that Roger's job was more important than Sharon's.

The more-or-less-equal partnership contract that had characterized roughly the first three years of their marriage, when both were in school or working full time, had slowly been replaced with a new contract which had a high potential for felt inequity on Sharon's part. Neither type of contract had truly been talked about and negotiated between the partners. Instead, practical circumstances (e.g., the need for an education, the desire to have a family, Roger's wish to get ahead) had dictated the contractual arrangements at any given time in the relationship. At this point, after roughly five years of marriage, the romantic ideals that had characterized their courtship and early relationship bonding seemed still to govern much of the marital interaction. Along these lines, Roger worked hard to become successful. At home (which was not actually vine covered or picket fenced but was, nonetheless, cozy), dutifully waiting for him at the end of the day were wife, daughter and, later, son. Sharon's career was an extra factor that did not comfortably fit with this romantic scenario and, therefore, could be accorded (by both partners) a lower priority than the other components. Somehow this situation did not feel quite right to Sharon, but she made the sacrifice in order to keep the family happy, and did not complain openly about the marital state of affairs.

Roughly two years after Doug was born, Roger was given tenure by the university. Sharon welcomed his promotion, and thought for certain that now Roger could provide more help with the couple's two children. Another critical event, occurring about the same time, was the offer to Sharon of a responsible, full-time position in the university's administrative hierarchy. Taking the position would mean a substantial increase in status and in income, since she would be working full time. After much soul-searching, and Roger's tacit, though not enthusiastic, agreement, Sharon decided to accept the offer. Pam was now in nursery school and a sitter was found for Doug. Roger, who had more time flexibility in his job, agreed to come home in the late afternoon to be with the children. Sharon was initially apprehensive about the new arrangements but, for the most part, things worked out and she eagerly pursued her new job.

At the time she entered therapy, Sharon had been working in the new position for about four years. Doug was now in nursery school and Pam was in the third grade. During the first conjoint therapy session, the therapist was interested in how the couple had structured their daily activities. This issue was brought up near the end of the session.

SESSION #1 (continued)

T: Could you say some more about your daily routine around the house? Who does what and how is it decided?

S: (to R) You want to start with that?

R: You go ahead.

S: Well, there's no set schedule, really. I usually get the kids ready in the morning and get breakfast. Roger drops them off at school. Then I straighten the house and go to work. The sitter's house is right by school. Doug just goes a half day and then he goes to the sitter for the afternoon. Roger comes by around three, picks up Doug and then goes home to be there in time for Pam. Then, I'm not sure, but I think he reads while the kids play, until I can get home to make supper. (Thinly veiled hostility is evident in Sharon's sarcasm at this point. This is the first hint that she may feel some inequity about the task distribution between her and Roger.)

S: (continuing) After supper, I play with the kids, or Roger does, and I usually do something that needs doing around the house. Then we put the kids to bed and read or watch TV for a while.

T: I see. It sounds a bit like you do have a schedule, even if it isn't a "set" one. How do you feel about the way things are divided up?

R: Seems fine to me. We've been doing it like that for a while.

T: Sharon?

S: Well, I'm glad Roger can come home early in the afternoon to be with the kids.

T: (to Sharon) Does the arrangement seem fair to you the way it is?

S: Well, it's not fifty-fifty, if that's what you mean. I do more of the things that need to be done around the house, but I've always done more.

T: (to Sharon) Is there any way you'd like to see things changed?

S: There's not a lot of time left for us at the end of the day. That bothers me. (Roger nods assent.)

T: Maybe we can talk more specifically about what changes would be helpful. You might want to begin thinking about that.

At this point, near the end of the first session, the therapist has the *hypothesis* that the couple's lack of time together may be related to Sharon's anger over the lack of felt support from Roger and the perceived inequity in domestic and child-care task distribution. Specifically, if she has angry feelings about such issues, spending more time together might well lead to her getting more in touch with these feelings and feeling the need to confront Roger with them. Both partners prefer to avoid such an angry confrontation. Thus, they may be limiting the degree of intimacy in the relationship, partly to avoid having to be angry with one another. In any case, the therapist has a sense of husband and wife collusion in this regard, e.g., despite her feelings, Sharon does continue to do more than her felt share of the work around the house. The therapist senses resistance on the part of the couple to the idea of plunging right in and dealing with these feelings. The therapist notes to himself that it is the resistance to direct expression of (particularly negative) feelings that may need to be worked on first in therapy.

The first session ends with the therapist suggesting (interpreting) to the couple that Sharon's job dissatisfaction may be compounded by some feelings of not being supported as completely as she would like in the marital relationship. Sharon agrees; Roger registers mild surprise, but does not overtly disagree (perhaps because he may have expected something along these lines when the therapist asked to see both spouses). The therapist then suggests that they begin meeting on a once-per-week basis to explore more completely this and other issues in the marriage. Roger wants to know how long it's going to take, and the therapist explains that he would like to meet somewhere between ten and fifteen sessions, and then see if further therapy was needed at that point. The couple agrees with this proposal and an appointment is set for the following week.

SESSION #2

After some initial pleasantries, the therapist is interested in how the couple has reacted to the suggestion that problems in the marital relationship may be related to Sharon's felt job dissatisfaction. The therapist is also concerned with moving therapy away from the idea that Sharon is the "identified patient" (the one with the problems) and toward the notion that each partner has some responsibility for the way things are in the relationship.

T: Did you have any reaction to our last session?

S: Not really. I mean, we talked some about it.

T: How did that go?

S: We talked about not having very much time together. And how maybe our communication has suffered because of that.

T: Say a little more about that.

S: Sometimes I feel like we're into our own worlds. I have my work; Roger has his. It's clear work is important for each of us, but I miss more going on between us.

T: (feeling the need at this point to bring Roger in) How do you feel about what Sharon is saying?

R: I feel we've grown apart some, but doesn't that happen at times to everybody who's married?

S: Yeah, but does it have to happen to us? It's too easy to say "it just happens" and let it go at that.

T: I wonder if there aren't some other things going on? Like maybe you're having some strong feelings that could be getting in the way of your communication. Are you aware of anything like that?

R: I think it's more a matter of time. If we take the time, we can usually talk things out. Like the weekend before last. We got a sitter and went out to dinner and talked and that was nice. (To Sharon) Wasn't it?

S: Yes.

T: Maybe I should rephrase the question then, in terms of whether you find yourselves taking the time?

S: Not often enough, for me. I don't really get the chance to say the things I want to. I let them build up, so that when we do talk, I've got a long list.

R: (smiling) A shit list, sometimes.

T: (to Roger) You're suggesting that Sharon is angry about some things. Any sort of regular things on that list that you're aware of?

R: She doesn't think I'm involved enough with the kids. But I'm with them quite a bit.

S: I'm not talking about the quantity of time you spend with them. It's the quality of time. I often have the sense you'd rather be reading or working rather than being with them.

R: Sometimes I do feel that way.

At this point, both partners have acknowledged a source of anger and frustration in the relationship. However, Sharon has focused her dissatisfaction on Roger's interaction with the children. This feels to the therapist like a possible displacement. Sharon may be more easily able to talk about Roger's withdrawal from interacting with the kids than about his withdrawal from interacting with her. There is still an avoidance of responsibility for angry feelings directed toward one another. Realizing that this avoidance of expressing anger may be a long-standing pattern for both individuals, the therapist decides on a structured communication task that might facilitate their each taking responsibility for the direct expression of such feelings. Toward the end of the session, this is introduced as follows:

T: I'd like you to try something during the coming week that might help open up communication a little more efficiently. I have a sense that you're reacting to the words of what each other is saying without listening so much to the feelings. You'll need about a half hour each day to do this. Try to pick a time when you're relatively free of distractions. Then I'd like one of you to talk for five minutes about a subject in the relationship toward which you have strong feelings. The other person is just to listen, and then during a second five-minute period repeat back what he or she heard the other person saying, particularly the feelings that seemed to be there. Then in the third five-minute period, the person who talked originally can tell the other whether he or she was correct in what they heard. Then, reverse things for the second fifteen-minute period and let the other person talk first. How would you feel about giving that a try?

S: Sounds worth doing.

R: Okay by me.

T: Do you have any questions about the procedure? (no questions) Try it for several days and you can let me know next time how it went.

SESSION #3

The couple started off by saying that they'd done their "homework" assignment only three times. (They seemed apologetic; the therapist, with lower expectations, felt this was a good start.) The discussion begins:

T: When you tried my suggestion, what kind of feelings came out?

R: Well, I became more aware of some of Sharon's frustration; with the job, with me . . . with us.

T: Do you share any of that frustration?

R: Yeah, I guess so. I mean, things haven't been too great since she started working full time. I feel like I'm being dumped on more.

T: Do you do any dumping back?

R: Not really, I usually keep things to myself. My life's a little smoother than hers now. At least at work.

T: (to Sharon) How do you feel about what Roger is saying?

S: I wish he'd share more. Sometimes he seems so damn self-contained. Then when I "fall apart" with feelings I feel guilty.

R: What do you want to know?

S: What you're feeling. About us. Are you worried about us? That we're getting distant?

R: Yes. But that's because you're so involved with your job right now.

S: I don't think that's the whole story.

T: (gently encouraging) What else could be involved?

S: I'm scared things are changing between us and I don't understand why.

T: Do you think your anger toward Roger is scaring you a little too?

S: Yes.

T: I have the sense that being able to feel comfortable being upfront about angry feelings is a problem for both of you. And my guess is that that comes somewhere from home—can you talk about how anger was dealt with in each of your families?

The rest of the session was spent in exploring the issue of the expression of anger in their families of origin. Both Sharon and Roger began to realize that direct communication of angry feelings was not truly modeled in either family of origin. The therapist took the position that, since frustration (and resultant anger) is inevitable in close relationships, people will either express these feelings directly or indirectly. He then suggested that the couple focus on how hostility was shown indirectly in their families of origin. This led eventually to the realization that both Roger and Sharon could more easily express anger directly toward their children than toward one another. The therapist toyed with the idea of bringing Pam and Doug in for a session but decided against doing so, since there was no definitive evidence that the children were symptomatically reactive at this point to the couple's problems.

SESSION #4

Continuing with the issue of expressing anger, the therapist pursued the hypothesis that the avoidance of direct expression of hostility served a mutually protective function. In this way, such behavior was an adaptive technique for the partners. About a third of the way through the session, this idea was presented.

T: To me, your not letting one another know directly when you're angry seems to be a protective device. A kind of mutual protective thing, since both of you seem to do it. Do you have any sense of that?

R: Well, I don't want to hurt Sharon by clobbering her with a lot of angry feelings. I mean, some of them can be pretty irrational.

T: We've been working on the notion that you'll let her see those feelings indirectly anyway. Do you have some sense that she can't handle your anger if you express it straight out? How do you think she might feel?

R: Hurt. I don't know, rejected maybe.

S: Yeah, I've felt that.

R: What?

S: Rejected. But I also feel that way when you withdraw.

T: Do you think both of you can feel pretty easily rejected, by each other? (Sharon nods, Roger is silent.) I think you may be particularly sensitive to that because of some previous experiences, with other people. Can you recall anything along these lines?

The rest of the session is spent exploring the residual feelings of rejection from the relationship Sharon had with Dan, and Roger had with Sue. The therapist points out that, because neither partner had many prior serious relationships, these two experiences may have left strong lasting impressions. The notion of their initial marital contract was then introduced. The therapist suggested that an implicit clause in the initial contract was along the lines of each not rejecting the other, because this had been such a painful experience in the past. It was pointed out that a correlate of this clause appears to have been that the spouses should not get directly angry with one another. To do so would lead to feelings of rejection and possibly reawaken painful past memories. The couple was instructed to focus on other facets of their initial relationship expectations and how these were affecting their present marital interaction.

SESSIONS #5 AND #6

Both these sessions were devoted to an elaboration of the initial marital contract and whether some of its provisions were in need of revision. This exploration helped Roger and Sharon to see that strong romantic ideals formed much of the basis for their early and continuing expectations of one another. Much of the

171

romance had gone out of the relationship, and this was painful to acknowledge. In some ways, the partners had withdrawn from one another rather than face openly the disappointment resulting from their changed perceptions. The withdrawal also served to preserve the romantic relationship in fantasy, without having to temper this conception unduly with reality.

At this point, the treatment strategy with Roger and Sharon had been similar to that which might have been used with any couple complaining of relationship dissatisfaction. First, an attempt was made to improve communication, with open disclosure of negative feelings especially stressed. Following this effort, the initial marital contract was explored, with an eye toward facets of the contract in need of revision. The relationship problems related to dual-career issues had not yet been dealt with specifically. In the therapist's judgment, it was necessary to lay the groundwork for exploring dual-career-related conflicts by first improving communication skills and focusing on initial marital contract issues.

SESSIONS #7 AND #8

Following the sixth session, the couple took a week's vacation, during part of which they visited Roger's parents. When therapy resumed, the therapist was particularly interested in the couple's reaction to this visit. The session began:

T: How was your vacation?

S: I think Roger enjoyed it a little more than I did. He likes being at his home and I must say I don't blame him—his mother treats him like a king. And they like to see the children.

T: Did you notice anything during the visit that seemed at all related to the things we've been talking about in here?

S: Well, like I said—I was reminded how Roger's mother dotes on him.

T: What does that mean for you?

S: I suppose it's obvious. I feel at times like he expects me to do the same.

T: Roger?

R: I suppose that's so. But you can't really compare the two.

172

We're not at my home very much, so naturally it's special for Mom when we're there.

T: (to Sharon) How have Roger's expectations along these lines affected the marriage?

S: I'm not sure.

T: I wonder if it's at all related to your feelings of doing more than what you feel is your share of things around the house, with the kids, and so forth?

S: I can see how that might be the case.

A discussion follows centering on Sharon's perception that, in some ways, Roger's career has been given a higher priority in the relationship than hers. For example, she has often "kept the kids quiet" so that he could work at home. Sharon feels angry about the frequency of these occasions and is beginning to feel more comfortable expressing such feelings directly to Roger. She also has some insight into his expectation that she take up in some ways where his mother left off, i.e., devote herself to his advancement, often at the expense of being able to put energy into her own career. It is becoming clearer to both how they have colluded in this process to carry on a pattern set up in Roger's family of origin. Session #8 further explores the feelings associated with this state of affairs, and how it has led Sharon to feel dissatisfied not only with her career, but also with the marriage.

SESSION #9

This session was focused on how the couple could begin changing their marital situation in the direction of a more equitable arrangement. Helping Sharon to feel a greater sense of relationship support for her career endeavors seemed a particularly important goal. This issue was introduced as follows:

T: I think we have a pretty good idea now where some of your feelings of dissatisfaction are coming from. I've heard Sharon, in particular, say that some things about your relationship don't feel quite fair. Maybe we could focus on how to go about changing that. Any ideas?

R: I remember a while back that you said something about whether we needed a more explicit schedule of who does what.

I didn't think we needed that at the time, but it's become clear why I would think that way—I guess I've had it pretty good. Anyway, maybe that's a place to start.

S: I agree. Then maybe we can see in black-and-white how things have been kind of uneven.

T: Do you have some thoughts about what needs to change?

S: I want Roger to help me more with the house. Especially since I do the cooking, and I'm willing to continue doing that. But there's no time for me after supper. There are things to do with the kids, and there is always a bunch of stuff around the house. You've got to realize I'm not one of these people who has to keep her house super neat and clean. I'm talking about just doing what needs to be done.

T: What bothers you the most about that?

S: I suppose it's that there's no time for myself. Roger has taken time for himself and I haven't. I can't really blame him for doing that. I haven't really asked for it up to now.

T: I think that's an important point. That you now seem more comfortable about asking directly for what you need. (to Roger) How do you feel about what Sharon is saying?

R: I think some adjustments are due. Perhaps I've been a bit selfish, in expecting the family to cater to my time demands.

T: Do you feel some resistance—inside—to making some of the changes Sharon seems to be asking for?

R: Honestly, yes (smiles).

T: It's been my observation that people—let's say, men, don't change in terms of sharing more of the load around the house, until their backs are up against the wall, so to speak. You know, we're really talking about sharing power—maybe "influence" is a better word—in the relationship.

S: I can see that. I want to feel that my wishes have as much influence on what we do as Roger's have. I don't feel it's been that way, up to now. But, like I said before, I haven't asked for it.

The rest of the session was devoted to exploring more explicitly how the couple might change their domestic task and child-care schedule in the direction of a more equitable distribution of responsibility. They were encouraged to negotiate and write out a schedule and then, if all went well, to give it a try before the next session.

SESSION #10

Roger and Sharon reported that they had worked out a schedule and, so far, their attempts to implement it seemed to be going fairly well. The therapist inquired whether each partner had scheduled in some time for himself or herself, as well as some regular time to be together as a couple. It seemed important to formalize (legitimize) these particular aspects of the schedule, since they related to additional specific problem areas that had been raised by the couple. Like most couples who try an explicit schedule for the first time, they felt their life was being regimented and programmed. This seemed to bother Roger more than Sharon, but he said: "I think I can live with it, at least give it a chance to work."

It seemed appropriate at this point to do a review of where things were in terms of the couple's presenting problems and whether there were additional areas that needed therapeutic work. Sharon indicated that the job pressures were still there, but stated: "I didn't really expect therapy to change that, since they're probably inherent in my work situation. People in middle management situations always seem to get the squeeze, from both above and below. At least that's what I've read." She went on to indicate, however, that she was feeling better about the marital relationship, adding: "I feel like Roger is really trying to help me out more. That's been nice. I didn't know if he'd be willing to change, and yet I knew something had to change. My blood pressure was a signal of that." Roger noted that Sharon seemed happier and that made him feel better about his efforts.

Roger indicated that he wanted to focus some on the couple's sexual relationship. He said that he would like more variety in their lovemaking, inferring that he felt Sharon to be somewhat sexually inhibited. She did not feel as dissatisfied as he, but did acknowledge that Roger had periodically brought up this issue. The therapist felt an exploration of prior sexual learnings, particularly what they had acquired in this regard from their families of origin, as well as any premarital sexual experiences, were important in understanding the background for any present felt difficulties. A review of prior experiences was begun toward the end of the tenth session and continued in the next meeting.

SESSION #11

Particularly important in understanding the partners' sexual relationship was the fact that their patterns of interaction had acquired rather fixed roles. Because Roger had had more premarital sexual experience, he had been defined by both spouses early in the relationship as Sharon's "teacher" in sex. She had been the "learner," who depended on Roger to introduce new techniques, initiate variety in lovemaking, etc. This pattern was congruent with Sharon's sexually repressive background and the conflicts engendered by such conditioning, in terms of whether she could be sexually assertive without feeling guilty. Adopting a relatively passive role in sex subconsciously permitted her to avoid taking responsibility for active fulfillment of her sexual needs.

For Roger, this sexual interaction pattern resulted in a frustration of his own wishes to, at times, adopt a passive role in lovemaking, i.e., the wish to lie back and be "acted upon" by an active, assertive sexual partner. He had not expressed these wishes directly to Sharon. However, when the therapist asked each spouse whether they had any persistent sexual fantasies, Roger reported a scenario in which an assertive, but gentle, woman excites him while he is in a helpless, somewhat restrained position. This fantasy revealed a wish for the sexual interaction roles in the marriage to be reversed at times, with Roger the passive "learner" and Sharon the active "teacher." Sharon had trouble sharing her sexual fantasies with Roger, and generally dismissed the request by saying: "Oh, they're pretty usual and mundane, when I have them. Once in a while I think of Paul Newman or Burt Reynolds, stuff like that (slightly embarrassed)."

The rigidity of fixed behavior roles characteristic of their sexual relationship mirrored to some extent the prior pattern in the marriage of Sharon "staying still" in her own (particularly, career) development while Roger actively advanced. This developmental pattern had begun to change in other areas of their life. The therapist surmised that their sexual relationship might also be open to modification along the lines of breaking up fixed patterns of interaction. It was suggested to Sharon that she might have some things to teach Roger about sex, and that he was seemingly receptive to learning. The couple were instructed to attempt a sexual interaction where Sharon was actively in charge and Roger was the recipient of her ministrations. They were told to carry this out to the degree that both felt comfortable with and that, if things stopped short of having intercourse, that was okay.

The therapist also suggested, as this was a new way of sexual relating, that the behaviors might seem a little unfamiliar at first, but probably would get more comfortable with practice.

Roger was somewhat more enthusiastic about the idea than Sharon, but she indicated a willingness to "give it a try." The differential response by the partners was not surprising, since the interaction suggested by the therapist was more congruent with Roger's sexual fantasies.

SESSION #12

The couple reported that they had tried out the therapist's suggestions and that things had gone well. Sharon was surprised, saying: "At first I thought, *Whatever can I teach him?* Then I realized that maybe it wasn't what we did, just that we were trying to do things differently." The therapist agreed. The rest of the session was spent talking about additional ways to introduce variety into the sexual relationship, as well as additional ways to free each partner from feeling locked into a certain, fixed pattern of sexual behavior. It was suggested that they talk more openly about what each liked the partner to do in terms of sexual arousal, in addition to letting each other know (gently) what was perhaps less pleasurable. Varying the place of lovemaking and sometimes acting out sexual fantasies—e.g., dressing up in "costume"—were also suggested as ways other people put variety into lovemaking. The emphasis was on talking with each other about what felt comfortable (and, hopefully, fun) to do and then feeling okay about doing it. The therapist realized that the repression of sexual feelings and wishes engendered by years of early social conditioning would not disappear overnight. Keeping this in mind, it seemed important nonetheless to give the couple permission from a perceived authority (parentlike) figure to be freer and more flexible in expressing affectional and sexual feelings. In addition, it was felt useful to let them know what other people, particularly those who had been married for some time, did sexually and what they found enjoyable. The emphasis in this instruction was on gentleness, noncoercion and sensitive understanding of the other person's feelings. The earlier therapeutic work, which had focused on opening up communication and facing angry feelings directly, was felt to be of potential benefit to the couple's physical relationship, by offering a means of clearing the air of hurts and grievances that can get in the way of comfortable affectional and sexual expression.

Toward the end of the twelfth session, Roger brought up the idea of ending therapy in the near future. He indicated that he and Sharon had talked about this and that she agreed. The therapist supported their wishes in this regard, saying: "I think we've covered most of the important areas, and there seems to be good evidence that things are changing for you. Why don't we meet one more time just to wrap things up and take care of loose ends? You might want to think about whether we haven't covered anything that's important."

SESSION #13

The couple reported feeling more sure of wanting to end therapy. The session was routine and pleasant. Sharon brought up the fact that she still found it hard to assert herself with superiors in her job situations, but that she was feeling a little more confident of being able to do this. The therapist suggested that things should get easier with practice and that being able to assert her demands and wishes in the marital relationship should have some carryover to the job situation. They asked a few questions about the therapist's life and family that had probably been on their minds for a while, e.g.: "How long have you been married? I assume those are your kids (pictured in the office)? Do you ever face problems like ours?" The questions were answered briefly but honestly by the therapist and the session ended cordially.

SESSION #14

Sharon phoned the therapist approximately seven months after the last session and stated, somewhat apologetically, that some of the "old problems" were reemerging and that she and Roger wished to come back to therapy. The therapist suggested that this was not an unusual experience for couples who had been in therapy and that, indeed, it might be a good idea to get together again.

During the session, it seemed clear that the couple had abandoned their formal schedule in regard to the sharing of domestic and child-care tasks and that this was once again working to Sharon's disadvantage. She had recently been home sick with a flu-like respiratory virus and was angry because Roger didn't take over and permit her to rest. He had been through a period of stress at work ("too damn many committees") and was feeling generally harried.

The therapist reiterated that each needed to state his or her expectations of one another openly during such periods of unanticipated disruption and then negotiate what each needed to do for the other. Roger stated (with a smile): "I knew that's what he (the therapist) was going to say." Thus, the additional session partly confirmed that the guidelines established in the earlier treatment period were still applicable for helping the relationship. The couple agreed that they needed to work out a new schedule and to spend more time talking directly about their expectations of one another. Along these lines, Sharon had still been thinking about the possibility of returning to graduate school and completing her doctorate. She intended to begin taking a couple of courses during the coming semester, four months away.

At the present time, a year and a half after the last session, the couple has not recontacted the therapist, and it is assumed that things are going well for them. This type of treatment course is a representative one for marital therapy, in that it was relatively short term and goal directed. There were several underlying personality themes in each partner that did not receive extensive focus due to time limitations. For example, Roger's underlying narcissistic expectation that he would be central in Sharon's life, in the same manner as he was in his mother's, was not explored fully. Sharon's underlying fears that asserting herself meant she was inherently "masculine" and that she had not completely resolved sexual identity conflicts, engendered by being a "tomboy" during much of her early developmental period, were not addressed in therapy. Instead, adaptive ways of behavior were emphasized, in which each partner might help the other meet or resolve these conflictual needs and expectations. For example, Sharon was supported in the idea that asserting herself and her wishes was entirely appropriate and, indeed, necessary, whether one was a man or a woman. In the sexual area, Roger was supported in his wish to lie back and be given special attention through Sharon's ministrations. Continued frustration of these underlying personality conflict areas remains potentially dysfunctional for the marriage. However, it is hoped that by making each partner sensitive to the other's vulnerability in such areas, the marriage itself can have a therapeutic effect over time.

·References·

ARNOTT, C. C. Husbands' attitude and wives' commitment to employment. *Journal of Marriage and Family,* 1972, *34,* 673–684.

ASTIN, H. *The woman doctorate in America.* New York: Russell Sage, 1969.

BAILYN, L. Career and family orientations of husbands and wives in relation to marital happiness. *Human Relations,* 1970, *23*(2), 97–113.

BAILYN, L. Family constraints on women's work. *Annals of the New York Academy of Science,* 1973, *208,* 82–90.

BARNETT, J. Narcissism and dependency in the obsessional–hysteric marriage. *Family Process,* 1971, *10,* 75–83.

BEBBINGTON, A. C. The function of stress in the establishment of the dual-career family. *Journal of Marriage and the Family,* 1973, *35,* 530–537.

BERMAN, E., SACKS, S. & LIEF, H. The two-professional marriage: A new conflict syndrome. *Journal of Sex and Marital Therapy,* 1975, *1*(3), 242–253.

BERMAN, E. M., MILLER, W. R., VINES, N. & LIEF, H. I. The age 30 crisis and the 7-year itch. *Journal of Sex and Marital Therapy,* 1977, *3,* 197–204.

BERNARD, J. Marriage: His and hers. *Ms.,* 1972, *1*(Dec.), 46.

BERNARD, J. *The future of marriage.* New York: Bantam Books, 1973, p. 36.

BLOOD, R. O. & WOLFE, D. M. *Husbands and wives: The dynamics of married living.* Glencoe, Ill.: Free Press, 1960.

BRYSON, R., BRYSON, J. B. & JOHNSON, M. F. Family size, satisfaction and productivity in dual-career couples. *Psychology of Women Quarterly,* 1978, *3,* 67–77.

BRYSON, R., BRYSON, J. B., LICHT, M. H. & LICHT, B. G. The professional pair: Husband and wife psychologists. *American Psychologist,* 1976, *31,* 10–16.

BURKE, R. J. & WEIR, T. Relationship of wife's employment status to husband, wife, and pair satisfaction and performance. *Journal of Marriage and the Family,* 1976a, *38*(2), 279–287.

BURKE, R. J. & WEIR, T. Some personality differences between members of one-career and two-career families. *Journal of Marriage and the Family,* 1976b, *38*(3), 453–459.

CUBER, J. F. & HAROFF, P. B. *Sex and the significant Americans.* Baltimore: Penguin Books, 1966.

DETRE, J. Mary Wollstonecraft and William Godwin: A revolutionary marriage. *Ms.,* 1972, *1*(Dec.), 78.

FEATHER, N. T. & RAPHELSON, A. C. Fear of success in Australian and American student groups: Motive or sex role stereotype. *Journal of Personality,* 1974, *42,* 190–201.

FELDMAN, S. Impediment or stimulant? Marital status and graduate education. *American Journal of Sociology,* 1973, *78,* 982–994.

FESTINGER, L. *A theory of cognitive dissonance.* Stanford, Calif.: Stanford University Press, 1957.

FOGARTY, M. P., RAPOPORT, R. & RAPOPORT, R. N. *Sex, career, and family.* Beverly Hills, Calif.: Sage, 1971.

FREUD, S. Some character types met in psychoanalytic work. Chapter 2. Those wrecked by success. *The standard edition of the complete works of Sigmund Freud.* London: Hogarth Press, 1916. Vol. 14, p. 316.

GARLAND, N. T. The better half? The male in the dual-profession family. In C. Safilios-Rothschild (Ed.), *Toward a sociology of women.* Lexington, Mass.: Xerox, 1972, 179–215.

GOTTMAN, J., NOTARIUS, C., GONSO, J. & MARKMAN, H. *A couples' guide to communication.* Champaign, Ill.: Research Press, 1976.

GRONSETH, E. Worksharing families: Adaptations of pioneering families with husband and wife in part-time employment. *Acta Sociologica,* 1975, *18,* 202–221.

GUERNEY, B. L. Filial therapy: Description and rationale. *Journal of Consulting Psychology,* 1964, *28,* 304–310.

GURMAN, A. S. & KNISKERN, D. P. Research in marital and family therapy: Progress, perspective and prospect. In S. L. Garfield & A. E. Bergin (Eds.), *Handbook of psychotherapy and behavior change,* 2nd ed. New York: Wiley, 1978.

GURMAN, A. S. & KNUDSON, R. Behavioral marriage therapy: I. A psychodynamic-systems analysis and critique. *Family Process,* 1978, *17,* 121–138.

HECKMAN, N. A., BRYSON, R. & BRYSON, J. B. Problems of professional couples: A content analysis. *Journal of Marriage and the Family,* 1977, *39*(2), 323–330.

HOFFMAN, L. W. Fear of success in males and females: 1965–72. *Journal of Consulting and Clinical Psychology,* 1974, *42,* 353–358.

HOLMSTROM, L. L. *The two-career family.* Cambridge, Mass.: Schenkman, 1972.

HOPKINS, J. & WHITE, P. The dual-career couple: Constraints and supports. *The Family Coordinator,* 1978, *27,* 253–259.

HORTON, M. Liberated women: Children? *Clinical Child Psychology Newsletter,* 1971, *10,* 710.

HUSER, W. R. & GRANT, C. W. A study of husbands and wives from dual-career and traditional-career families. *Psychology of Women Quarterly,* 1978, *3,* 78–89.

JOHNSON, C. L. & JOHNSON, F. A. Attitudes toward parenting in dual-career families. *American Journal of Psychiatry,* 1977, *134*(4), 391–395.

KAPLAN, H. S. *The new sex therapy.* New York: Brunner/Mazel, 1974.

KARPEL, M. Individuation: From fusion to dialogue. *Family Process,* 1976, *15,* 65–82.

KLEIN, D. P. Women in the labor force: The middle years. *Monthly Labor Review,* 1975 (Nov.), 10–16.

LEDERER, N. J. & JACKSON, D. B. *The mirages of marriage.* New York: Norton, 1968.

LEIN, L. ET AL. Final report: Work and family life. National Institute of Education Project No. 3-3094. Cambridge, Mass.: Center for the Study of Public Policy, 1974.

MARSHALL, J. R. The expression of feelings. *Archives of General Psychiatry,* 1972, *27,* 786–790.

MARTIN, T. W., BERRY, K. J. & JACOBSEN, R. B. The impact of dual-career marriages on female professional careers: An empirical test of a Parsonian hypothesis. *Journal of Marriage and the Family,* 1975, *37*(4), 734–742.

MILLER, S., NUNNALLY, E. W. & WACKMAN, D. B. *Alive and aware: Improving communication in relationships.* Minneapolis: Interpersonal Communication Programs, 1975.

MONAHAN, L., KUHN, D. & SHAVER, P. Intrapsychic vs. cultural explanations of "fear of success" motive. *Journal of Personality and Social Psychology,* 1974, *29,* 60–64.

MURSTEIN, B. Stimulus–value–role: A theory of marital choice. *Journal of Marriage and the Family,* 1970, *32,*465–481.

NADELSON, T. & EISENBERG, L. The successful professional woman: On being married to one. *American Journal of Psychiatry,* 1977, *134,* 1071–1076.

PALOMA, M. Role conflict and the married professional woman. In C. Safilios-Rothschild (Ed.), *Toward a sociology of women.* Lexington, Mass.: Xerox, 1972.

PALOMA, M. M. & GARLAND, T. N. The married professional woman: A study in the tolerance of domestication. *Journal of Marriage and the Family,* 1971, *33,* 531–540.

PARSONS, T. *Essays in sociological theory.* Glencoe, Ill.: Free Press, 1954.

PLONE, A. Marital and existential pain: Dialectic in Bergman's "Scenes from a Marriage." *Family Process,* 1975, *14,* 371–378.

RAPOPORT, R. & RAPOPORT, R. *Dual-career families.* London: Penguin Books, 1971.

RAPOPORT, R. & RAPOPORT, R. N. Men, women and equity. *The Family Coordinator,* 1975, *24,* 421–432.

RAPOPORT, R., RAPOPORT, R. N. & THIESSEN, V. Couple symmetry and enjoyment. *Journal of Marriage and the Family,* 1974, *36*(3), 588–591.

RICE, D. G., RAZIN, A. M. & GURMAN, A. S. Spouses as co-therapists: "Style" variables and implications for patient–therapist matching. *Journal of Marriage and Family Counseling,* 1976, *2,* 55–62.

RICE, D. G. & RICE, J. K. Non-sexist marital therapy. *Journal of Marriage and Family Counseling,* 1977, *3,* 3–10.

RICE, J. K. & RICE, D. G. Status and sex-role issues in co-therapy. In A. S. Gurman & D. G. Rice (Eds.), *Couples in conflict: New directions in marital therapy.* New York: Aronson, 1975, pp. 145–150.

RIDLEY, C. A. Exploring the impact of work satisfaction and involvement on marital interaction when both partners are employed. *Journal of Marriage and the Family,* 1973, *35*(2), 229–237.

ROSEN, B., JERDEE, T. H. & PRESTWICH, T. L. Dual-career marital adjustment: Potential effects of discriminatory managerial attitudes. *Journal of Marriage and the Family,* 1975, *37*(3), 565–572.

ROSOW, J. & ROSE, K. D. Divorce among doctors. *Journal of Marriage and the Family,* 1972, *34,* 587–598.

SAFILIOS-ROTHSCHILD, C. The dimensions of power distribution in the family. In H. Grunebaum & J. Christ (Eds.), *Contemporary marriage: Structure, dynamics, and therapy.* Boston: Little, Brown, 1976.

SAGER, C. J. *Marriage contracts and couple therapy.* New York: Brunner/Mazel, 1976.

SAGER, C. J., KAPLAN, H. S., GUNDLACH, R. H., KREMER, M., LENZ, R. & ROYCE, J. The marriage contract. *Family Process,* 1971, *10,* 311–326.

ST. JOHN-PARSONS, D. Continuous dual-career families: A case study. *Psychology of Women Quarterly,* 1978, *3,* 30–42.

SALZMAN, L. *The obsessive personality.* New York: Aronson, 1973.

SHEEHY, G. *Passages: Predictable crises of adult life.* New York: Dutton, 1976.

SMITH, J. W. & GRUNEBAUM, H. The therapeutic alliance in marital therapy. In H. Grunebaum & J. Christ (Eds.), *Contemporary marriage: Structure, dynamics, and therapy.* Boston: Little, Brown, 1976, pp. 353–370.

STAINES, G. L., PLECK, J. H., SHEPARD, L. J. & O'CONNOR, P. Wives' employment status and marital adjustment: Yet another look. *Psychology of Women Quarterly,* 1978, *3,* 90–120.

STEINGLASS, P. The conceptualization of marriage from a systems theory perspective. In T. J. Paolino & B. S. McCrady (Eds.), *Marriage and marital therapy: Psychoanalytic, behavioral and systems theory perspectives.* New York: Brunner/Mazel, 1978, pp. 298–365.

STEWART, R. H., PETERS, T. C., MARSH, S. & PETERS, M. J. An object-relations approach to psychotherapy with couples, families, and children. *Family Process,* 1975, *14,* 161–177.

TOOMIM, M. Structured separation with counseling: A therapeutic approach for couples in conflict. *Family Process,* 1972, *11,* 299–310.

WALLSTON, B. S., FOSTER, M. A. & BERGER, M. I will follow him: Myth, reality, or forced choice: Job seeking experiences of dual-career couples. *Psychology of Women Quarterly,* 1978, *3,* 9–21.

WALSTER, E., WALSTER, G. W. & BERSCHEID, E. *Equity: Theory and research.* Boston: Allyn and Bacon, 1978.

WEINGARTEN, K. The employment pattern of professional couples and their distribution of involvement in the family. *Psychology of Women Quarterly,* 1978, *3,* 41–52.

WEISS, R. L. Contracts, cognition and change: A behavioral approach to marriage therapy. *The Counseling Psychologist,* 1975, *5,* 15–26.

WEISS, R. L. The conceptualization of marriage from a behavioral perspective. In T. J. Paolino & B. S. McCrady (Eds.), *Marriage and marital therapy: Psychoanalytic, behavioral and systems theory perspectives.* New York: Brunner/Mazel, 1978, pp. 165–239.

WEISS, R. L., BIRCHLER, G. R. & VINCENT, J. P. Contractual models for negotiation training in marital dyads. *Journal of Marriage and the Family,* 1974, *36,* 321–330.

Index

Index

time demands and, 56
use of work to avoid, 56
with other people, 61

Jackson, D. B., 41, 183
    183
Jacobsen, R. B., 1, 15, 34, 65,
    68, 183
Jealousy, 61
Jerdee, T. H., 1, 184
Johnson, C. L., 10, 31, 49–51,
    150, 183
Johnson, F. A., 10, 31, 49–51,
    150, 183
Johnson, M. F., 33, 69, 181

Kaplan, H. S., 43, 183–84
Karpel, M., 112, 183
Klein, D. P., 6, 183
Kniskern, D. P., 90, 94, 133,
    140, 182
Knudson, R., 112, 182
Kremer, M., 184
Kuhn, D., 115, 183

Lederer, N. J., 41, 183
Lein, L., 3, 183
Lenz, R., 184
Licht, B. G., 69, 181
Licht, M. H., 69, 181
Lief, H. I., 2, 31, 72–73, 181
Living together:
    implied contract in, 2
    stress of, 2

Marital satisfaction:
    adaptive patterns and, 67
    degree of, 150
    duration of marriage and,
        33
    husbands and, 67

perceived inequity and, 103
personality characteristics
    and, 42
optimizing strategies for,
    144–52
with "work-sharing,"
    151–52
Marital therapist:
    activity level of, 93–94, 101
    agenda of, 92
    attitudes and biases of,
        95–97
    as catalyst, 116
    collusion and, 96
    defenses used by, 97–99
    experience level of, 134
    parental transference and,
        134, 136–37
    personal conflicts of, 96–97
    as role model, 133
    skills of, 90
    "style," in co-therapy, 134,
        138
    theoretical orientation of,
        95
    transference and, 134
    values of, 93, 95
Marital therapy; see also
    Therapeutic technique(s)
    affective components of,
        98–99, 113
    agendas, 92
    career issues and, 93
    communication skills in,
        117, 129
    conjoint treatment format
        of, 90, 140
    co-therapy and, 97
    defenses used in, 97–98
    difference with other
        therapies, 90–95

Rice, J. K., 4, 95, 123, 125, 138, 184
Ridley, C. A., 1, 184
Role(s):
  change in, 1
  competition for, 68
  deviance in, dual-career wives, 32
  division of, in marriage, 74
  fixity of, 17
  gender expectations and, 4, 8, 71, 75, 96, 103, 115, 128, 152
  historical aspects of, 7–10
  of "mentor," 17–19
  strain in, 50–51, 67–68, 88, 150
Rose, K. D., 72, 184
Rosen, B., 1, 184
Rosow, J., 72, 184
Royce, J., 184
Russia, 87

Sachs, S., 1, 31, 72–73, 181
Safilios–Rothschild, C., 80, 87, 184
Sager, C. J., 4, 10, 24, 27, 43, 93, 104–105, 127, 139–40, 184
Salzman, L., 27, 38, 184
Scenes from a Marriage, 60–61
Separation, marital, 141
Sexual relationship(s):
  extramarital factors and, 23
  with other individuals, 61–62
  power issues and, 82
  problems in, 18–19, 23–24, 42–47, 82, 93, 175–76
  sharing fantasies and, 176

stereotyped roles in, 42–43, 176–77
variety and, 177
"work-sharing" and, 151–52
Shaver, P., 115, 183
Sheehy, G., 16, 184
Shepard, L. J., 3, 150, 185
Smith, J. W., 92, 184
Social change:
  marriage and, 71–72
  women and, 71–72
Social life:
  friendship patterns of, 60, 111
  relationships with others and, 60–62, 73, 111
  restriction of, 60–61
  work and, 60–61
Social role; *see* Role(s)
"Splitting," as defense, 52
Staines, G. L., 3, 33, 150, 185
Steinglass, P., 90, 185
St. John–Parsons, D., 19, 31–33, 50, 56, 87, 150, 184
Stewart, R. H., 52, 54, 106, 185
Success neurosis, 123
Support system, marital:
  "back-up" for, 88
  child-care in, 3, 22, 33, 48, 56, 150–51
  conflicts around, 36, 87–90
  and domestic tasks, 3–4, 8–10, 22–23, 56, 69, 87–88
  and emotional needs, 3, 31, 45, 55, 160
  occupational tasks and, 34–35, 45
  therapeutic help with, 89, 128–29